Geurst & Schulze Architecten

Editorial

Vor mir liegt das Manuskript des nahezu fertigen Buchs über die Bauten der Architekten Geurst & Schulze aus Den Haag. In mich versunken lasse ich meinen Blick von Seite zu Seite wandern. Ich lese im Text von Charles Rattray, der darin eindrücklich nachzeichnet, was die Architekten berührt und bewegt, und wo ihre architektonischen Wurzeln liegen. Daneben das klare, einprägsame Bild einer Gebäudefassade mit acht gleich grossen Fensteröffnungen, die präzise in das Ziegelstein-Fugenbild eingepasst sind. Auf der nächsten Doppelseite wird der Text begleitet von einem beruhigend wirkenden Bild eines überhohen Gangs mit einem linienförmigen Oberlicht an der Decke, im Hintergrund eine Zwischenwand mit bewusst gesetzten, von Holz gefassten Glaselementen. Mein Blick schweift weiter zu den Projektseiten, wo sich Text, Pläne und Bilder ergänzen, wobei bisweilen der Text im Vordergrund steht, bisweilen die Bilder und wiederum auf einzelnen Seiten die Pläne. Während dieses stillen, achtsamen Betrachtens kommen mir die Gedanken Paul Valérys in den Sinn, der 1926 in den *Notes sur le livre et le manuscrit* schreibt: «So ist das Buch einerseits imstande, durch seine *Deutlichkeit* eine Bewegung auszulösen und fortzuleiten – eine Bewegung, die diskontinuierliche intellektuelle Wirkungen hervorbringt und die nach und nach die Zeile entlang in Gedanken aufgeht; andererseits ist es ein *Gegenstand*, eine Gesamtheit *bleibender* Eindrücke, mit unmittelbaren, *von keiner Übereinkunft festgelegten* Eigentümlichkeiten ausgestattet, die geeignet ist, unser sinnliches Wohlgefallen oder Missfallen zu erregen.» Dann streifen die Bilder der Bauten von Jeroen Geurst und Rens Schulze meinen Blick, und ich finde in den Projektdarstellungen bestätigt, dass in ihrer Architektur ein Faszinosum liegt, da sie Ruhe und Unaufgeregtheit ausstrahlt und – gleichsam im Unsichtbaren – erfüllt ist von Erfindungen im Grossen wie im Kleinen. Diese Erfindungen liegen verborgen in den Qualitäten des Raums, den der Erscheinungsform und der Plastizität der Bauten, der Grundriss- und Schnittentwürfe, der Massregulierungen, der städtebaulichen Ordnungen, der lebensnahen Tauglichkeit und schliesslich der Materialien und Farben. Sie gilt es auf den folgenden Seiten zu entdecken.

Luzern, im Juni 2013 Heinz Wirz

Editorial

The manuscript of the almost completed volume on buildings by the architects Geurst & Schulze from The Hague lies before me. I silently move my eyes from side to side as I study it in depth. I read the text by Charles Rattray, who impressively describes what touches and moves the architects and where their architectural roots lie. Beside that text, I regard the clear, striking image of a building façade with eight equally sized window apertures that are precisely inserted into the brickwork and mortar form. On the next double page, the text is accompanied by an image with a calming effect, an extra-high walkway zone with a linear-shaped ceiling light. In the background a partition wall has carefully-positioned glass elements set in wood. My view wanders further to the projects, where the text, plans and images complement each other, so that sometimes the text is in the forefront, while at others the images and full-page plans dominate. During this silent, attentive observation, thoughts of Paul Valéry come to mind, who wrote in his *Notes sur le livre et le manuscrit* in 1926: "So on the one hand, the book is able through its *explicitness* to cause and drive forwards a movement – a movement that yields discontinuous intellectual effects and that gradually dissolves in thought along the line. On the other hand, it is an *object*, a unity of *lasting impressions*, equipped with *no generally agreed* peculiarity, that is suitable for engendering our sensory pleasure or disapproval." My eyes wander further over the images of buildings by Jeroen Geurst and Rens Schulze and I read in the project descriptions about the fascinating aspect of the peace and calmness that their architecture radiates, as well as – even in invisible aspects – being filled with architectural inventiveness, both great and small. These inventions are hidden in the qualities of the space, the qualities of the formal appearance and the sculptural nature of the buildings, the ground plans and the cross-sectional designs, as well as the regulation of scale, the urban planning order, the practically-oriented suitability and finally the materials and colours. This book allows you to discover all of those aspects.

Lucerne, June 2013 Heinz Wirz

Geurst & Schulze Architecten
Den Haag

Quart Verlag Luzern

Geurst & Schulze Architecten
7. Band der Reihe De aedibus international/Volume 7 of the series De aedibus international

Herausgeber/Edited by: Heinz Wirz, Luzern
Konzept/Concept: Geurst & Schulze Architecten, Den Haag; Heinz Wirz
Textbeitrag/Article by: Charles Rattray, Aberdeen
Objekttexte/Project descriptions: Geurst & Schulze Architecten
Vorwort/Foreword: Heinz Wirz
Übersetzung aus dem Holländischen ins Englische/Translation Dutch into English: Susan Hunt, *Plain English*, Leidschendam
Übersetzung aus dem Englischen/Translation into German: Christian Rochow, Berlin
Textlektorat Deutsch/Text editing German: Leni Lopez, Berlin
Fotos/Photos: Stefan Müller, Berlin S./p. 11, 40–54, 57 (5, 7), 58 (10), 59 (12); Christian Richters, Berlin S./p. 7, 9, 12–39, 57 (4), 58 (8, 9, 11), 59 (13, 14); Geurst & Schulze Architecten S./p. 41 (Innenansicht/interior), 46 (links/left), 47, 59 (15), 61; Piet Rook, Rotterdam S./p. 56 (1, 2, 3), 57 (6); Michiel Sablerolle, Gouda S./p. 60
Visualisierungen/Graphics: DPI, Den Haag S./p. 55
Grafische Umsetzung/Graphic design: Quart Verlag, Linus Wirz
Lithos: Printeria, Luzern
Druck und Bindung/Printing and binding: DZA Druckerei zu Altenburg GmbH

Quart Verlag GmbH
Denkmalstrasse 2, CH-6006 Luzern
books@quart.ch, www.quart.ch

Bauen im Kontext: Korrespondenzen und Zwänge

Charles Rattray*

Im Akt des Bauens offenbart sich die Architektur. Wird diese praktische und bodenständige Tätigkeit von Prinzipien geleitet und von kritischer Imagination beflügelt, so wird das Alltägliche zum Aussergewöhnlichen. Darum war für Konrad Wachsmann die Konstruktion der Wendepunkt und für Mies van der Rohe Architektur die Kunst des Bauens. Dieser alchemistische Vorgang hat zwei anspruchsvolle, direkte Konsequenzen: zum einen eine nicht zu übergehende physische Präsenz, die die Umgebung modifiziert und gleichzeitig von ihr modifiziert wird, und zum anderen eine metaphorische Verortung, einen Platz im Kontinuum der Architekturgeschichte. In beiden Bereichen bringt das gebaute Werk die bestehende Ordnung in Bewegung, kommentiert deren Tradition und nuanciert unser Verständnis von Vergangenheit und Gegenwart. Auf dieser kräftigenden Wechselseitigkeit beruht der kulturelle Diskurs.

Die Arbeiten von Geurst & Schulze nehmen scheinbar zwangsläufig und mühelos ihren Platz in dieser Kultur der Architektur ein – was nicht heissen soll, dass sie auch zwangsläufig und mühelos zustande kommen, denn eine wichtige Voraussetzung ist eine gute Kommunikation und Zusammenarbeit zwischen Architekt, Bauherr, Bauunternehmer, Stadt, Gesellschaft und Nutzer (die Liste liesse sich noch erweitern), die einhergeht mit unzähligen Entscheidungen, Interpretationen und Urteilen. Worauf nun stützen sich die Einsichten dieser Architekten? In welchen – physischen und intellektuellen – Kontexten stehen ihre architektonischen Ideen?

Kein Kontext ist so entscheidend wie die geologische Beschaffenheit eines Ortes, und dies gilt auch und vor allem für die Niederlande. Deren natürliche Oberfläche ist die eines Flussdeltas: Sie besteht aus Sand und Lehm (Materialien, die sich nicht dadurch auszeichnen, dass sie Lasten besonders gut aufnehmen). Aber die Menschen haben in die Geologie stark eingegriffen und selbst Boden geschaffen in Form von Poldern, die dem Meer abgewonnen wurden und durch Dünen und Deiche vor Fluten geschützt sind. Wir können ausser Acht lassen, dass niederländische Bauingenieure aufgrund dieser Bedingungen im Laufe der Jahrhunderte ein beträchtliches Wissen über Pfahlgründungen und den Umgang mit Grundwasser angehäuft haben (weshalb die Kirchtürme in diesem Land trotz aller Senkungsbewegungen gerade gen Himmel streben), und uns auf zwei Punkte von unmittelbarer architektonischer Relevanz konzentrieren. Der erste ist die Palette an verfügbaren Baustoffen, in der Naturstein kaum vorkommt und die vom rein Organischen zu einer Konzentration auf Holz und Backstein führte. Der zweite Punkt ist die radikale Idee der Geländeumgestaltung, aufgrund derer niederländische

Construction, Correspondence and Constraint

Charles Rattray*

It is in the act of *building* that architecture shows itself. When this practical and down-to-earth skill is guided by principles and nourished by critical imagination, the normal becomes noble. That is why for Konrad Wachsmann, construction was its turning point and why for Mies van der Rohe, architecture was its art. There are two direct and challenging consequences of this alchemic process: the first is an ineluctable physical presence modifying, and being modified by, what surrounds it on shared ground; the second is a metaphorical location, a place in the continuum of architectural history. In both, the built work stimulates the existing order, comments on its tradition and nuances our understanding of both the past and the present. In this invigorating reciprocity lies cultural discourse.

The works of Geurst & Schulze take their place in this architectural culture with apparent inevitability and effortlessness – which is to say that there is nothing either inevitable or effortless about it, but rather that the establishing of a nexus between architect, client, builder, city, society and user (the list might continue) has demanded innumerable choices, interpretations and judgments. What feeds their discernment? What are the contexts – both physical and intellectual – of their architectural ideas?

No context is more fundamental than the geology of a place, and in the Netherlands this is remarkable. The natural surface layer is that of a river delta: sand and clay (neither known for its load-bearing capacity). But man has been an important geological agent, actually constructing a considerable proportion of the surface geology in the form of the polders, reclaimed from the sea and protected from it by dunes and dykes. We may leave to one side the notable facts that Dutch engineers over the centuries have, as a consequence of these conditions, developed considerable expertise in dealing with ground-water and with pile foundations (which is why steeples of Dutch churches continue to rise vertically, against all the odds of subsidence) and instead focus on two thoughts with immediate relevance for architecture. One is a palette of vernacular building materials that has almost no natural stone and that developed from the purely organic to became one of timber and brick; a second is the radical idea of a changed ground, as a result of which Dutch architects think as much in terms of constructing the landscape as of working within it.

On sand or on clay, brick remains the quintessential building material in the Netherlands. This is despite a post-Second World War interest in building systems and the same wide availability of innumerable building materials as anywhere else. Brick endures because

* Charles Rattray (1956) studierte Architektur an der Universität von Edinburgh und war zwanzig Jahre als Architekt tätig, unter anderem im Büro von Sir Leslie Martin. Charles Rattray ist Dozent an der Universität von Dundee und einer der Lektoren der *Architectural Research Quarterly* (Cambridge University Press). Gemeinsam mit Andrew Peckham und Torsten Schmiedeknecht war er Herausgeber des Bandes *Rationalist Traces* (London, New York: Wiley, 2007).

* Charles Rattray (1956) studied architecture at the University of Edinburgh and worked in practice for twenty years including a period with Sir Leslie Martin. He is a Senior Lecturer at the University of Dundee and an Editor of *Architectural Research Quarterly* (Cambridge University Press). With Andrew Peckham and Torsten Schmiedeknecht, he edited *Rationalist Traces* (London, New York: Wiley, 2007).

Architekten nicht nur in der Landschaft bauen, sondern auch immer gleich daran denken, sie zu gestalten.

Für Gebäude auf Sand- oder Lehmboden war Backstein von jeher das wichtigste Baumaterial in den Niederlanden. Das gilt auch heute noch, trotz des Interesses am Fertigteilbau seit dem Ende des Zweiten Weltkriegs und trotz der Tatsache, dass in den Niederlanden wie überall sonst unzählige andere Baumaterialien zur Verfügung stehen. Der Backstein behauptet sich wegen seiner Nützlichkeit, weil er schön altert, und schlicht auch wegen seiner Allverfügbarkeit. Auch in den Arbeiten von Geurst & Schulze tritt er immer wieder in Erscheinung. Wie der Stahlbetonrahmen und wie industrielle Bauverfahren gehört der Backstein zu ihrer Formensprache, die nicht immer frei ist von Pragmatismus und finanziellen Zwängen. Zugleich aber ist Backstein ein Material, das auf einzigartige Weise dem bestehenden Gefüge der Stadt entspricht.

Der Begriff *Entsprechung* impliziert, dass vorhandene Merkmale eines Ortes verstärkt oder neu präsentiert werden. Für Geurst & Schulze bedeutet dies

of its utility, because it weathers so well, and simply because of its ubiquity. We see it again and again in the work of Geurst & Schulze, too. Like the concrete frame and industrialised building techniques, it is a part of their vocabulary that is informed by pragmatism and financial constraint, but it is also a part uniquely able to correspond with the fabric of the existing city.

The term *correspond* carries with it the implication of extending or re-presenting known characteristics of a place. For Geurst & Schulze this is more than a straightforward opposition to tabula rasa Modernism and more than a simple commentary on a city's morphology; it extends to a passion – one might say a ruling passion – for the history of architectures both grand and humble. This is what T. S. Eliot meant when he wrote:

"the historical sense compels a man to write not merely with his own generation in his bones, but with a feeling that the whole of the literature of Europe from Homer and within it the whole of the literature of his own country has a simultaneous existence and composes a simultaneous order."[1]

[1] T. S. Eliot, 'Tradition and the Individual Talent', in Selected Prose of T. S. Eliot, ed. Frank Kermode (London: Faber and Faber, 1975), p. 38

Bürogebäude 2. Hafen, Scheveningen, Den Haag, 2003

Office building, 2nd Harbour Scheveningen, The Hague, 2003

7

1 T. S. Eliot: Tradition and the Individual Talent. In: Selected Prose of T. S. Eliot. Ed. Frank Kermode. London: Faber and Faber 1975. S. 38

2 Adam Caruso, The Feeling of Things (Barcelona: Polígrafa, 2008), p. 19
3 Ibid. p. 41

2 Adam Caruso: The Feeling of Things. Barcelona: Polígrafa 2008. S. 19
3 Ebd. S. 41

mehr als einen klaren Widerspruch zum Tabula-rasa-Modernismus und mehr als einen schlichten Kommentar zur städtischen Morphologie; sie fühlen geradezu eine Passion – manch einer würde dies auch eine besessene Leidenschaft nennen – für die Geschichte der Architektur, gleichgültig, ob es sich um repräsentative oder bescheidene Bauten handelt. Im gleichen Sinne meinte T. S. Eliot, dass in der Literatur der historische Sinn dafür sorge, dass der Autor nicht nur als Vertreter seiner Generation schreibe, sondern dass die gesamte europäische Literatur seit Homer und vor allem die gesamte Literatur seiner Muttersprache im Akt des Schreibens präsent sei und eine simultan existierende Ordnung bilde.[1]

Der Blick durch dieses Prisma des historischen Wissens gibt Geurst & Schulzes Interpretation und kritischer Bewertung der Variablen, denen sie sich in dem jeweiligen Projekt stellen, ihre besondere Qualität; doch ist es die kreative Arbeit selbst, die diesen Blick auf das Schaffen analoger Bedingungen und die Herstellung historischer Kontinuität richtet. Dabei handelt es sich niemals um beiläufige Anspielungen, sondern um neue Schöpfungen, die über Architekturen der Vergangenheit reflektieren und uns daran erinnern, dass in der Architektur, wie in vielen kulturellen Disziplinen, die besten Interpretationen von Kunst selbst Kunst sind.

Wenn Rossis Formulierung «l'architettura sono le architetture» (die man mit «Architektur ist das Produkt vergangener Architekturen» umschreiben könnte) in diesem Zusammenhang einschlägig ist, dann können wir auch Adam Carusos Bemerkung über die inhärente emotionale Qualität der Architektur zustimmen. Er schrieb, dass L'architettura della città (die Architektur der Stadt) betone, «wie das architektonische Material, die vertrauten Formen der Gebäude, Strassen und Plätze der europäischen Stadt […] auf einer grundsätzlichen, weithin zugänglichen, gefühlsmässigen Ebene operierten»[2]. Anderswo formulierte er, dass das «nie endende Potential der Stadt wenig mit Neuheit und theoretischer Abstraktion zu tun hat, sondern in der tief berührenden Welt der Dinge verhaftet ist»[3]. Deutlich zeigt sich dieses gefühlsmässige Verständnis in der Poesie, bei der es Gemeingut ist, den Lesern vertraute Erfahrungen zu präsentieren (oder neu zu präsentieren); weniger ersichtlich ist es in der Architektur, die gewissermassen gezwungen ist, für sich selbst zu sprechen. Geurst & Schulze beweisen, dass es auch anders geht: Bei ihnen verdrängen die Notwendigkeiten der jeweiligen Bauaufgabe scheinbar niemals die Forderungen der Stadt in ihrer Gesamtheit, und die praktische Ökonomie ihres Rationalismus setzt niemals das Verständnis ausser Kraft, dass es schliesslich darum geht,

Seeing things through this prism of historical knowledge gives a very distinctive quality to Geurst and Schulze's interpretation and critical evaluation of the variables that confront them in any project; but it is the creative work itself that focuses these towards the making of analogous conditions and a historic continuity. This is never a casual allusion but a fresh creation that reflects on past architectures and reminds us that, as in so many cultural disciplines, the best readings of art are art.

If Rossi's phrase, "l'architettura sono le architetture" (which may be translated as "architecture is the product of past architectures") is part of this, then we may also agree with Adam Caruso's reminder of its inherent emotional quality when he notes that L'architettura della città (The Architecture of the City) emphasised "how the material of architecture, the familiar forms of vernacular structures, the streets and squares of the European city [...] operated at a fundamental and a widely accessible, emotional level"[2] and, elsewhere, his observation that "[the] never-ending potential of the city has little to do with novelty and theoretical abstraction but is held within the deeply moving world of things".[3] This is an emotional understanding well demonstrated by poetry, where the presenting (or re-presenting) of familiar experience for others is a stock-in-trade; it is much less easily discovered in architecture, which must somehow speak for itself. Nevertheless, Geurst & Schulze, for whom the necessities of the individual building programme never seem to outweigh the imperatives of a collective urban condition, and for whom the practical economy of their Rationalism never outweighs the sense that they are, at the end of the day, making "rooms" with rich interior qualities, prove otherwise. To understand this through just one example, look at how the Vermeer Tower in Delft – a significant urban mark that was part of a planning strategy for the city – "collects" the gardens of the adjacent terraces in its courtyard and, internally, makes a series of places of pronounced yet open-handed character. I especially recall one of these, the day-centre for the elderly whose dado-paneled ground-floor gallery, with finely curtained tall windows to the court moderating light reminiscent of Vermeer's casements, has a quality of "home" that is extraordinary – initially because it seems so completely appropriate for the old; then even more extraordinary when one discovers that the programme for that part was originally a kindergarten. There is a generosity in this programmatic adjustment as well as a demonstration that formal qualities in this sort of work go far beyond the aesthetic. It shows that buildings can be emotional understanding in action. Such things may seem remote from the systematic

Räume von hoher Qualität zu schaffen. Ein Beispiel dafür ist, wie der Vermeertoren in Delft – ein auffälliges städtisches Wahrzeichen, entstanden im Zusammenhang eines Stadtplanungsprojekts – die Gärten der umliegenden Häuserreihen in seinem Hof «versammelt» und drinnen eine Reihe von Orten mit ausgeprägtem, aber leicht erzieltem Eigencharakter erschafft. Ich erinnere dabei besonders an das Seniorenzentrum. Die unteren Wandflächen seines ebenerdigen Saals sind mit Holz vertäfelt, die in den Hof blickenden grossen Fenster sind schön mit Vorhängen versehen, die das Licht so dämpfen, dass man an die Fensterbilder Vermeers erinnert wird und ein ausgesprochen «heimeliges Gefühl» entsteht, wie Senioren es lieben. Dass diese Gestaltung so gelungen ist, überrascht umso mehr, wenn man erfährt, dass das Programm hier ursprünglich einen Kindergarten vorgesehen hatte. Im Umgang mit dieser programmatischen Änderung liegt eine gewisse Grosszügigkeit, die aber auch beweist, dass formale Qualitäten, wie sie in dieser Arbeit zutage treten, nicht unbedingt auf dem Anspruch reiner Ästhetik beruhen, und dass ein Gebäude sehr wohl ein in die Tat umgesetztes Verständnis der Gefühle anderer sein kann.

Derartige Sachverhalte scheinen der systematischen Ordnung und dem präzisen Determinismus, die man mit dem rationalen Bauen verbindet, fernzustehen, doch verhält es sich genau umgekehrt: die expressive Erfindungskraft von Geurst & Schulze hängt von den formalen und materiellen Zwängen ab, wird von diesen freigesetzt und entfaltet sich in der Arbeit an ihnen. Beispiele für dieses faszinierende Paradox finden sich in allen Künsten. Georges Perec schrieb einen Roman in seiner französischen Muttersprache, bei dem keine Wörter mit dem Buchstaben «e» zulässig waren; Vikram Seth schrieb – nicht ganz so extrem – seinen ersten Roman in vierhebigen Sonettstrophen; Johann Sebastian Bachs *Wohltemperiertes Klavier* besteht aus zwei Sätzen von 24 Präludien und Fugen in den zwölf Halbtönen der chromatischen Tonleiter, jeweils in Dur und Moll. Giorgio Morandi malte fast vierzig Jahre lang immer wieder die gleichen Flaschen und Töpfe. Und Palladios obsessives Interesse für harmonische Proportionen ist so vertraut, dass es fast schon ein Klischee ist.

Jeroen Geursts Faszination für solche Zwänge zeigt sich in seiner wegweisenden Untersuchung über die Gedenkstätten, die Lutyens für die gefallenen Soldaten des Ersten Weltkriegs errichtete.[4] Nachdem die Grundprinzipien des Entwurfs für die Gedenkstätten und Soldatenfriedhöfe festgelegt waren, führte der tragisch gewaltige Umfang des Auftrags zu einer enzyklopädisch umfassenden Erkundung der Variationsmöglichkeiten des Ursprungsentwurfs bei den

order and precise determinism associated with Rational building but in fact it is precisely the opposite: the expressive inventiveness of these architects is *dependent* on constraints both formal and material – is liberated by them and operates through them. This fascinating paradox is demonstrable in all the arts. Consider Georges Perec, who wrote a novel in his native French while denying himself the use of the letter "e", or, more reasonably, perhaps, Vikram Seth who wrote his first novel in tetrameter sonnet-stanzas. J. S. Bach's *Das Wohltemperierte Klavier* (the Well-Tempered Clavier) consists of preludes and fugues that follow the 12 semi-tones of the chromatic scale in both major and minor keys. Giorgio

Vermeer Tower, Seniorentagesstätte/day-centre for the eldery, Delft, 2007

[4] Jeroen Geurst: Cemeteries of the Great War by Sir Edwin Lutyens. Rotterdam: 010 Publishers 2010

4 Jeroen Geurst, Cemeteries of the Great War by Sir Edwin Lutyens (Rotterdam: 010 Publishers, 2010).

5 Peter Carter: 'Mies van der Rohe: An Appreciation on the Occasion. This Month, of His 75th Birthday'. In: Architectural Design 31/3. März 1961. S. 97

5 Peter Carter, 'Mies van der Rohe: An Appreciation on the Occasion, This Month, of His 75th Birthday', in Architectural Design 31/3 (March 1961), p. 97

jeweiligen Gedenkstätten. Ein ähnliches Prinzip zeigt sich bei Geurst & Schulze auch am anderen Ende der Grössenskala: bei ihrem Interesse für das Standardmass niederländischer Ziegel, das nach dem gleichnamigen Fluss benannte Waalformat von 21 x 10 x 5 cm. Sie betrachten drei Backsteinlagen als äquivalent mit einer Treppenstufe (bzw. 18,5 cm) und 16 Stufen (bzw. 48 Ziegel) als die Entsprechung der Geschosshöhe einer Wohnung. Bei Projekten wie dem Amsterdamer Andreas Ensemble schreiten sie fort zu Pfeilerbreiten von sieben Sturzsteinen und Feldern, die sieben Pfeilerbreiten oder 49 Sturzsteinen entsprechen. Andere würden hier schlicht von einer Länge von 5,4 Metern sprechen, aber Geurst & Schulze treiben das Prinzip bis zu den nicht aus Ziegeln bestehenden Elementen (Fensterteilungen usw.) fort, so dass das gesamte Gebäude – das eine kombinierte Typologie darstellt – von einem einzigen System durchdrungen und vereint wird. Ob wir das erkennen, ist eine Frage, die wir genauso gut in Hinblick auf Palladio stellen könnten, doch sei daran erinnert, dass Mies van der Rohe beim Anblick von Berlages Amsterdamer Börse nach eigener Aussage «die Idee der klaren Konstruktion als einer der Grundprinzipien, die wir akzeptieren sollten», kam. Darüber, fuhr Mies fort, liesse sich leicht diskutieren, aber die Umsetzung sei schwierig. Es sei sehr schwer, sich an dieses grundlegende Konstruktionsprinzip zu halten und dann ein Gebäude hochzuziehen. «Mit der Struktur haben wir eine philosophische Idee. Die Struktur ist das Ganze, von oben bis nach unten, bis ins letzte Detail – alles geformt von der gleichen Idee.»5

Durch einen glücklichen Zufall liegt das von Berlage entworfene und 1935 fertiggestellte Gemeentemuseum Den Haags nur zwanzig Gehminuten von den Büroräumen von Geurst & Schulze entfernt. Auch in seinem letzten Werk verwandte Berlage wiederum ein durchgängiges Konstruktionsprinzip. Doch während es sich bei der Börse um einen Monolithen aus tragendem Ziegelmauerwerk handelte, präsentiert sich das Museum als eine Synthese verschiedener Elemente und Materialien – Betonrahmen, Backsteinverkleidung und verschiedenen Verkleidungen im Inneren – was die Umsetzung erschwerte. Um dieses zu lösen blickte Berlage in die Schriften seines geistigen Mentors Gottfried Semper, der darauf verwiesen hatte, wie eine Stoffbahn, aufgehängt an dem Gerüst einer primitiven Behausung, für die Einfriedung des Raumes sorgen kann. Damit hatte er ein Verfahren beschrieben, wie sich in den Worten von Edward R. Ford «ein rationales Gebäude mittels analoger konstruktiver Systeme durch Verkleidungsmaterialen verwirklichen liesse, die genau

Morandi painted the same bottles and pots repeatedly for almost forty years. Palladio's preoccupation with harmonic proportion is familiar to the point of cliché.

Jeroen Geurst's fascination for this was beautifully demonstrated in his definitive study of Lutyens' Great War cemeteries.4 Once the principles of the cemetery designs had been agreed, the tragically large scale of the commission resulted in an encyclopaedic exploration of variations on the original theme. From innumerable examples in Geurst's practice, we may choose one from the other end of te scale: their interest in the format of the standard Dutch Waal brick (named after the river), which measures 21 x 10 x 5 centimetres. Geurst and Schulze enjoy thinking in terms of three brick courses being equal to one step of a stair (or 18.5 cm), and 16 steps (or 48 bricks) being a domestic storey-height; then, at the Andreas Ensemble in Amsterdam, for example, they progress to pier widths of seven headers and bays equivalent to seven piers, or 49 headers. Others might call this 5.4 metres, but here the discipline goes on into non-brick components (window divisions and so on) such that the entire building – and it is a combined typology – is permeated and united by a single system. Whether we see this or not is the same question we might ask of Palladio, but it reminds us of Mies van der Rohe's description of Berlage's Exchange in Amsterdam:

"The idea of clear construction came to me there, as one of the fundamentals we should accept. We can talk about it easily but to do it is not easy. It is very difficult to stick to this fundamental construction, and then to elevate a structure. [...] By structure, we have a philosophical idea. The structure is the whole, from top to bottom, to the last detail – with the same idea."5

By a happy coincidence, a twenty-minute walk in the right direction through the streets of The Hague brings you from the offices of Geurst & Schulze to Berlage's Municipal Museum, completed in 1935. In this, his last work Berlage again addressed ways of expressing a consistent construction but whereas the Exchange is a monolith of load-bearing brickwork, the museum is a synthesis of different elements and materials – a concrete frame, brickwork cladding and varying interior finishes – and the problem is correspondingly more difficult. In resolving it Berlage turned to the writing of his mentor, Gottfried Semper, who had written a woven wind-break hung on the wooden frame of a primitive structure to provide enclosure. In so doing he described a way in which "rational building could be achieved by means of analogous structural systems, by finish materials that describe

die konstruktiven Systeme beschreiben, die sie verhüllen»[6]. Und so finden wir in dem Museum eine wie ein Gewebe – Semper hätte von «Flechtwerk» gesprochen – eingesetzte Ziegelverkleidung, die den Betonrahmen und die Folge der schön gegliederten Räume umhüllt. Ausgehend von den angepassten Backsteinmassen von 20 x 10 x 4,5 cm (Backsteinfans wissen vor allem letztere Dimension zu schätzen!) entwickelte Berlage einen Raster von 1,1 m. Die Untersuchungen von Jeroen Geurst zeigen, dass Berlage die Masse des Backsteins allen Elementen des Bauwerks, bis hinunter zu den Ausstellungsvitrinen, zugrunde legte.

Für Geurst & Schulze ist dieses Gebäude ein Lehrbeispiel, ja fast ein Talisman, und die geographische Nähe eine Metapher für Verbindungen auf geistiger, tektonischer und städtischer Ebene. Wie Berlage erfreuen auch sie sich an konstruktiver Logik und sind von der Vorstellung einer Dekoration fasziniert, die gleichsam natürlich aus den Konstruktionsverfahren erwächst. Dabei sind sie der Geschichte der Architektur und der historischen Kontinuität in der Stadt verhaftet. Vor allem aber teilen sie die Überzeugung, dass sich die Architektur im Akt des Bauens zeigt.

the true structural systems they conceal" as Edward R. Ford put it.[6] And so we have the woven appearance – Semper might have called it *wickerwork* – of non-structural brickwork at the Museum that wraps concrete frame and encloses a succession of finely-wrought, roof-lit, spaces. There too, from an adjusted brick size of 20 x 10 x 4.5 (and how brick-fanciers will enjoy that last dimension!) Berlage established a 1.1 metre grid. Jeroen Geurst's research has shown that he extended the brick sizing to every area of the building, right down to the display cases.

For Geurst & Schulze this building stands as an object-lesson, a talisman almost, and the easy geographical connection serves as a metaphor for links that are intellectual, tectonic and urbane. Like Berlage, they relish structural logic and are fascinated by the idea of decoration arising quasi-naturally through construction methods; they are immersed in the history of architecture and absorbed by the historical continuity in the city. But above all, they share the belief that it is in the act of building that architecture shows itself.

[6] E. R. Ford: The Details of Modern Architecture. Cambridge, Mass: The MIT Press 1990. S. 205

[6] E. R. Ford, The Details of Modern Architecture (Cambridge, Mass: The MIT Press, 1990), p. 205

Wohnanlage Meeuwenhof, Den Haag, 2010

Meeuwenhof residential housing, The Hague, 2010

Viertes Anmeldezentrum, Ter Apel

Fourth Registration Centre, Ter Apel

Entwurf/Design: 1999–2000
Ausführung/Construction: 2000–2001
Bauherrschaft/Client: Staatlicher
Gebäudedienst/Government Building
Agency

Auszeichnung/Award: Shortlist Mies
van der Rohe Award 2003

In diesem Gebäude finden die ersten Befragungen von Asylbewerbern statt, die eine Aufenthaltsgenehmigung für die Niederlande beantragen. Der Komplex besteht aus zwei Teilen: einem Bestandsgebäude, in dem die Verwaltung untergebracht ist, und einem Neubau, in dem die Asylsuchenden ein paar Tage zubringen. In dieser Zeit werden sie mehrfach von Beamten der Einwanderungsbehörde zu ihrem Fall befragt. Das Gebäude umfasst Aufenthalts- und Schlafräume für die Asylsuchenden sowie Befragungszimmer und Büros für die Beamten der Ausländerbehörde, der niederländischen Polizei, des Flüchtlingswerks und der Einwanderungsbehörde. Das Anmeldezentrum, das gleich hinter dem Dorf Ter Apel in der Nähe zur deutschen Grenze liegt, wurde auf dem Gelände eines früheren Materialdepots der NATO errichtet. Das neue Gebäude ist von Klosteranlagen inspiriert, wie sie an Landesgrenzen häufig anzutreffen sind. Der zweigeschossige Bau beruht auf einem viereckigen Grundriss mit vier Innenhöfen. Die kühle Strenge der Aussenfassaden ist dem Wunsch geschuldet, das Gebäude nicht allzu einladend erscheinen zu lassen. Das Innere präsentiert sich hingegen offen und licht, um den Asylsuchenden den Aufenthalt so angenehm wie möglich zu machen. Verbunden werden die beiden Teile des Komplexes durch einen hohen Gang von perspektivischer Wirkung. Angesichts der kurzen Entwurfszeit von zwei Monaten und der knapp kalkulierten Bauphase von elf Monaten wurde entschieden, für die Konstruktion ein leicht demontierbares Fertigteil-Bausystem zu verwenden; dieses umfasst ein Stahlskelett, Betonhohldielen und vorgefertigte hölzerne Innenwandschalen. Als Verkleidung für die Fassade mit ihren Aluminium-Fensterrahmen wurden Keramikfliesen gewählt, die im Farbton dem Lehm der umliegenden Landschaft entsprechen.

It is in this building that the initial interviews with asylum-seekers applying for a Dutch residence permit take place. It has two parts: a previously existing building which houses the management, and a new building where the asylum-seekers spend a few days. During this period they have a number of interviews with staff of the Immigration and Naturalisation Service (IND). The building has waiting rooms and sleeping areas for asylum-seekers, as well as interview rooms and offices for officials of the Aliens Department, Royal Netherlands Military Constabulary, the Dutch Refugee Council and the Immigration and Naturalisation Service (IND). The building is situated just outside the village of Ter Apel, close to the German border, on the grounds of a former NATO storage depot. The new building was inspired by a monastery: a type of building which has often been sited close to national borders. It has a square ground plan with four courtyards and is made up of two storeys. The introverted outward appearance of the building was in response to the desire not to make it too inviting. The interior, by contrast, is open and light to make the asylum-seekers' stay as pleasant as possible. The two parts of the building are linked by a high corridor which tapers in both height and with, thereby creating a perspective effect. The short design period of two months and the very short construction time of 11 months meant that a prefabricated, easily disassembled construction system had to be used, comprising a steel frame, concrete channel floor units and prefabricated wooden inner leaves. The façade has aluminium window frames with ceramic elements in the clay colour of the surrounding landscape.

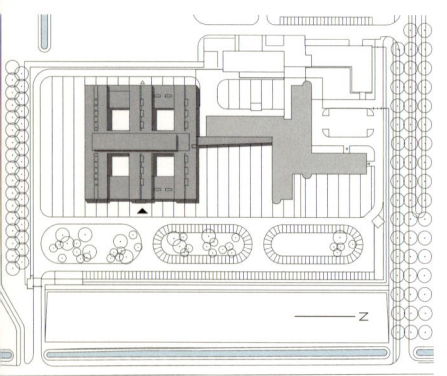

4

13

11

15

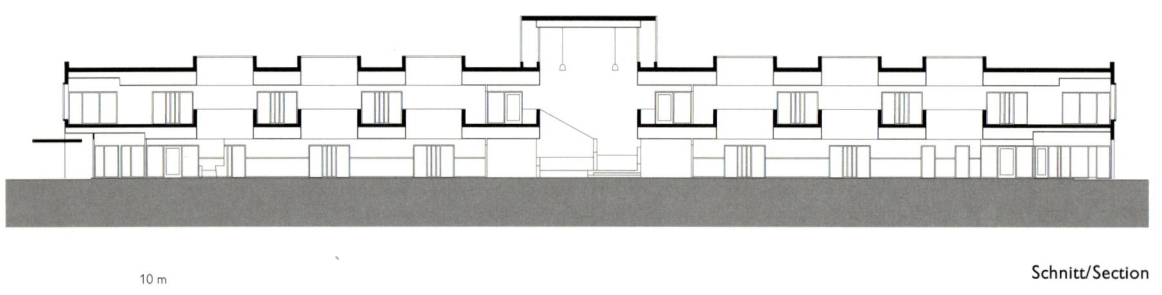

10 m

Schnitt/Section

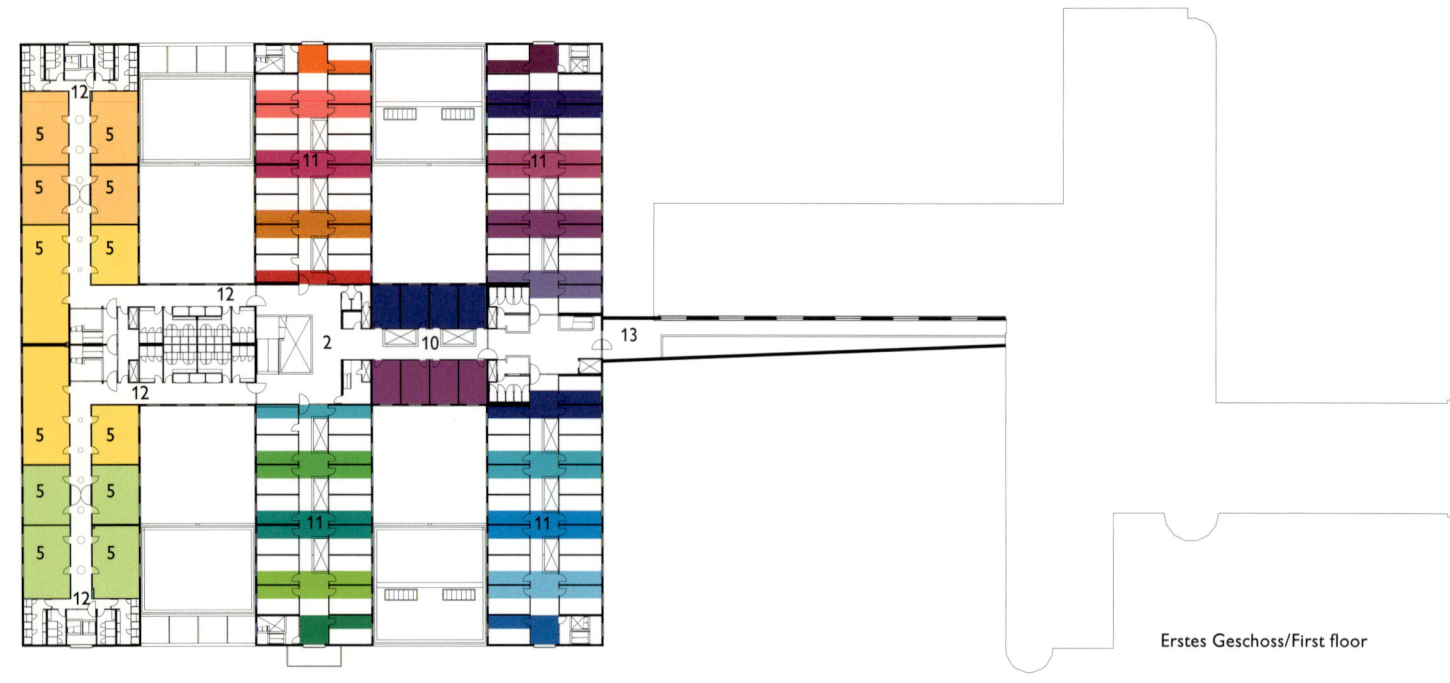

Erstes Geschoss/First floor

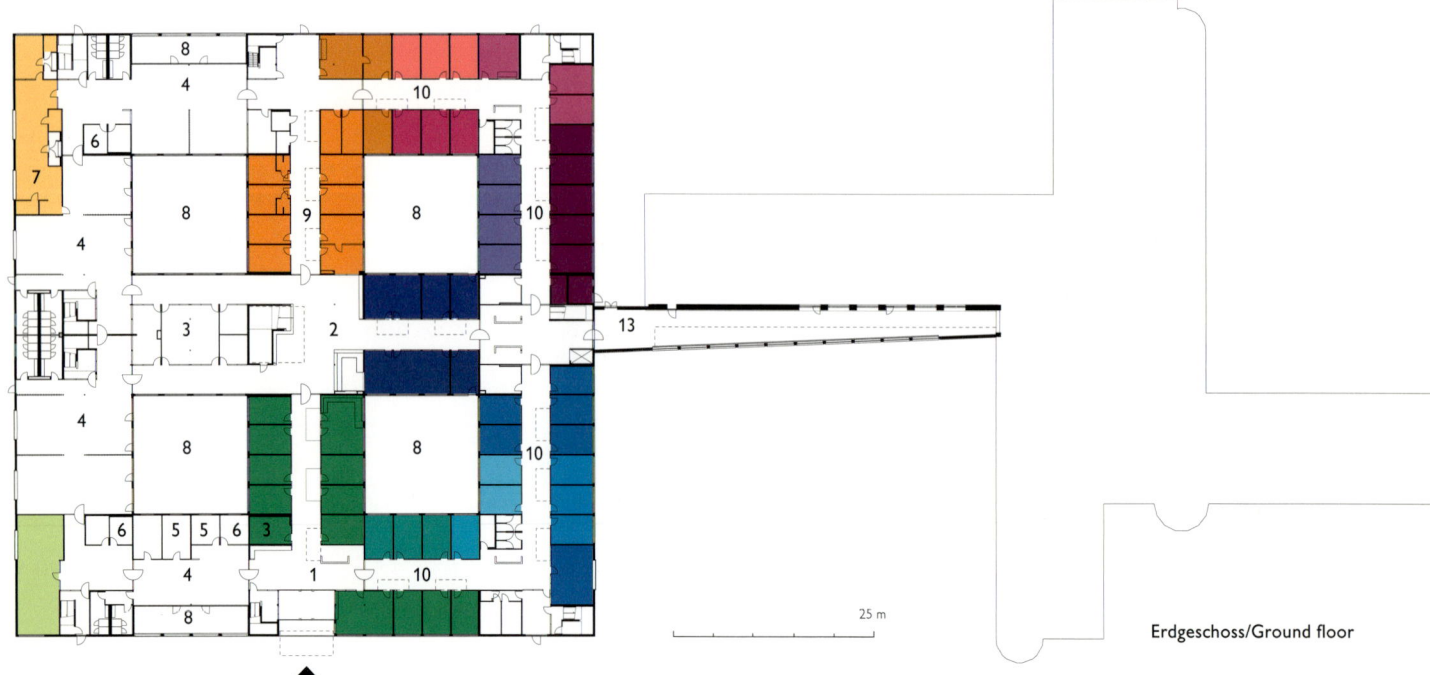

25 m

Erdgeschoss/Ground floor

16

11

1 Eingang
2 zentrale Halle/Haupttreppenhaus
3 Garderobe
4 Wartesaal
5 Schlafsaal
6 Meditationsraum
7 Kinderkrippe
8 Hof
9 Medizinische Versorgung
10 Büro
11 Befragungsraum
12 Duschen/Toiletten
13 Verbindungsgang zum Bestandsgebäude

1 Entrance
2 Central hall/main staircase
3 Luggage
4 Waiting room
5 Dormitory
6 Mediation space
7 Crèche/Childcare
8 Courtyard
9 Medical service
10 Office
11 Interview rooms
12 Shower/Toilets
13 Passage to excisting building

10

17

Stadtvillen und Bürogebäude Scheveningen Hafen, Den Haag

Urban Villas and Offices Scheveningen Harbour, The Hague

Entwurf/Design: 1997–1999
Ausführung/Construction: 2001–2002
Bauherrschaft/Client: Delta Lloyd
Vastgoed, Malherbe de Juvigny
Vastgoed BV

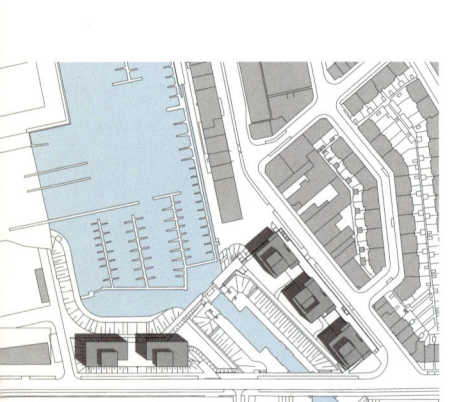

An der Spitze des Zweiten Hafens entstanden zwei Bürogebäude und drei Stadtvillen. Das Baugelände befindet sich in der Nähe eines Schleusenkomplexes, der als Siel dient, um überschüssiges Wasser aus dem Hinterland in den Hafen gelangen zu lassen. Der Hafen wurde in einem ursprünglichen Dünengebiet angelegt. Die Neubauten sind so platziert, dass sie den Hafen und den Schleusenkomplex einfassen, ohne die Offenheit des Geländes zu beeinträchtigen. Die beiden Bürogebäude haben jeweils vier Geschosse über einer gemeinsamen Tiefgarage. Die Eingänge liegen an einem Freiplatz zwischen den Gebäuden, von dem aus man einen guten Blick auf den Hafen hat. Im Inneren sind die Decken der Büroräume mit schallisolierenden, frei abgehängten Holzpaneelen verkleidet; im Kern der Gebäude, der die Technik- und Toilettenräume enthält, wurden die Wände ebenfalls mit Holz verkleidet. Die drei Stadtvillen sind zum Schleusenkomplex hin ausgerichtet; jede verfügt über eine eigene Tiefgarage. Über den Tiefgaragen verläuft ein öffentlicher Fussweg, an dem die Eingänge liegen. Pro Etage gibt es vier Wohnungen. Im obersten Geschoss befinden sich je zwei Penthousewohnungen. Eine von ihnen umfasst zwei Etagen, die über ein Atrium miteinander verbunden sind. Die Gebäude wurden architektonisch so konzipiert, dass sich von jeder Wohnung Ausblicke auf den Hafen ergeben. Sowohl die Bürogebäude als auch die Stadtvillen zeigen aussen eine robuste Backsteinverkleidung und grosse, tief liegende Fenster, wie sie für Bauten in einem Hafenviertel von jeher typisch sind. Rund um die Gebäude wurde in Erinnerung an den Ursprung des Geländes Dünenvegetation angepflanzt.

Two office buildings and three urban villas with apartments were designed and built at the head of the Second Harbour. The site is next to a lock complex which also acts as a sluice, draining surplus water from the hinterland into the harbour. The harbour was built in what was originally a dune landscape. The building volumes define the harbour and the lock complex on the one hand but do not detract from the openness of the area on the other. The two office buildings consist of four storeys each built over a shared parking garage. The entrances to the two buildings are on a communal plaza between the buildings, which also provides a good view of the harbour. The urban villas each have their own garage and are oriented towards the lock complex. There is a public footpath over the garages where the entrances are also situated. There are four apartments on each storey. The top floor comprises two penthouses, one of which has a second storey. These are linked by an atrium. The typology of the buildings means that every apartment has a view of the harbour. Both the offices and the residential buildings have been finished in robust brick with large, deep-set windows, in keeping with the architectural style that is typical of the harbour. Dune vegetation has been planted around the buildings, also reflecting the origins of the area.

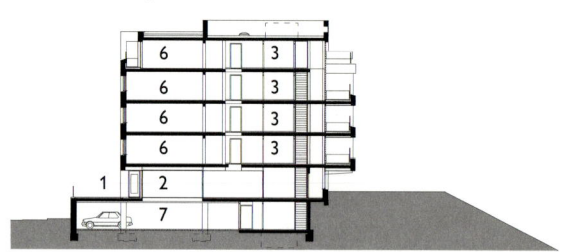

Schnitt/Section

1	Öffentlicher Fussweg	1	Public path
2	Eingang zu den Wohnungen	2	Entrance to the apartments
3	Aufzugshalle	3	Lift lobby
4	Büro Erdgeschoss	4	Office groundfloor
5	Lager	5	Storage
6	Wohnung	6	Apartment
7	Garage	7	Car park

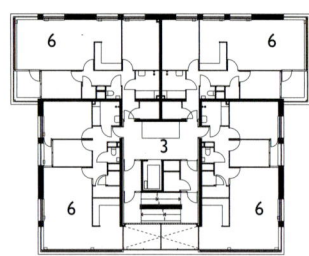

Erstes Geschoss/First floor

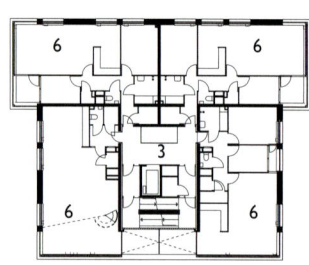

Drittes Geschoss/Third floor

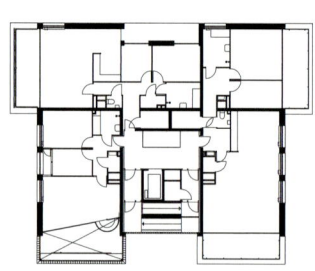

Viertes Geschoss/Fourth floor

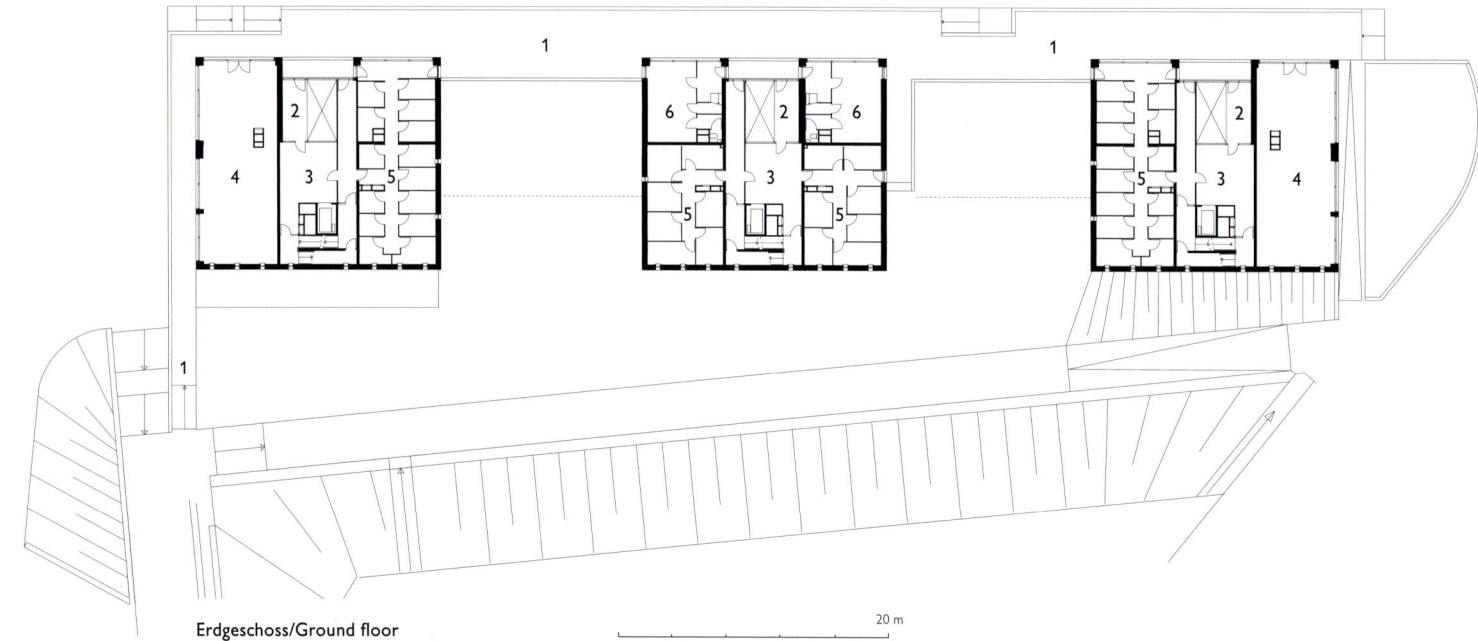

Erdgeschoss/Ground floor

20 m

20

1 Gemeinsam genutzte Plaza
2 Eingang
3 Aufzugshalle
4 Büro
5 Garageneinfahrt
6 Garage

1 Communal plaza
2 Entrance
3 Lift lobby
4 Office
5 Entrance car park
6 Car park

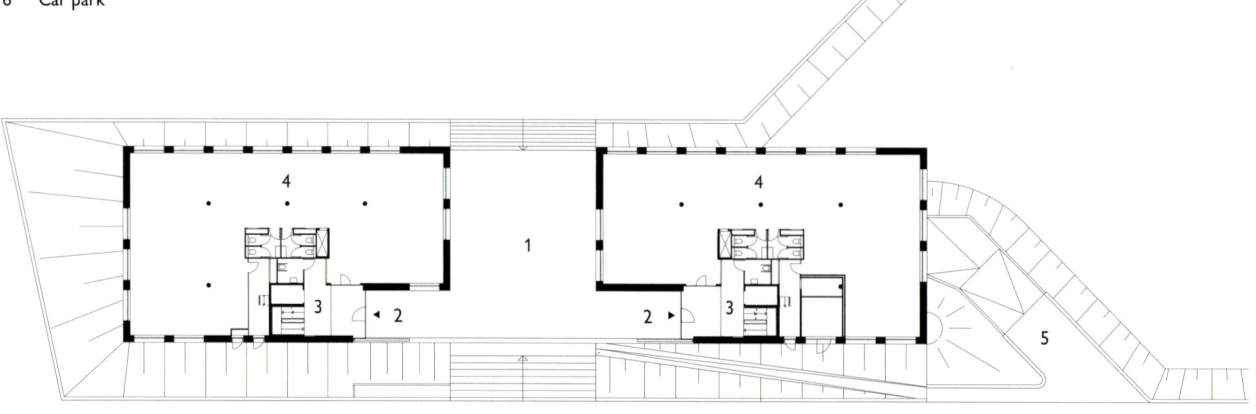

Erdgeschoss/Ground floor

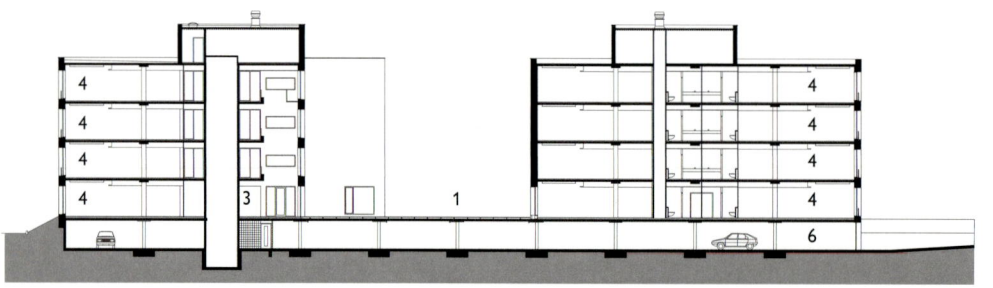

Schnitt/Section

Villenpark Trompendael, Hilversum

Trompendael Villa Park, Hilversum

Entwurf/Design: 1999–2001
Ausführung/Construction: 2003–2005
Bauherrschaft/Client: V.O.F. Villapark Trompendael

Auf einem ehemaligen Landgut unmittelbar nördlich von Hilversum wurden 24 Wohnhäuser errichtet. Das Areal grenzt an ein exklusives Wohnviertel, für das sehr strenge Bebauungsrichtlinien gelten, die sich auch auf das Volumen der Neubauten und die Neigung ihrer Dächer erstreckten. Um zu verhindern, dass die Häuser durch die Einhaltung dieser Richtlinien traditionell anmuten, wurde ihre Form weitgehend abstrakt gehalten. Für die Dächer und Fassaden wurden möglichst einheitliche Materialien ausgewählt. Dem Entwurf der Häuser liegt ein quadratischer Grundriss und ein einfaches Satteldach zugrunde. Dieses Modell wurde sowohl für die frei stehenden als auch für die Reihenhäuser verwendet. Bei den Reihenhäusern wurden die Dachkanten gegeneinander gedreht, um jedem Haus eine unverwechselbare Note zu geben. Der auf einem modularen System beruhenden Grundkonstruktion wurden schliesslich noch Erker und Dachgauben hinzugefügt, durch die jedes Haus einzigartig wirkt. Diese Differenzierung wird dank der vier verschiedenen Farben, die für die einzelnen Gebäude gewählt wurden, noch zusätzlich betont. Aufgrund des vorhandenen Gefälles auf dem Grundstück – eine Seltenheit in den Niederlanden – war es möglich, unter den Häusern Tiefgaragen unterzubringen.

24 houses were built on a former country estate just north of Hilversum. The estate bordered on an exclusive residential area with very restrictive planning rules. The planning regulations specified the volume and roof angle required for the new houses. To prevent these regulations imposing a traditional style of architecture, the built structures were made as abstract as possible. The roofs and façades were made consistent with one another by using th same materials and colour. The main design of the houses was based on a square ground plan with a simple saddle roof. This model design was built in both detached and terraced forms. For the terraced houses, the roof ridges were turned relative to one another to make each house distinctive. Dormers and bay windows were then added to this basic structure based on a modular system, ultimately making each house unique. This was further emphasized by the four different colours used for each building. The height differences on the site – unusual for the Netherlands – meant that garages could be built under the properties.

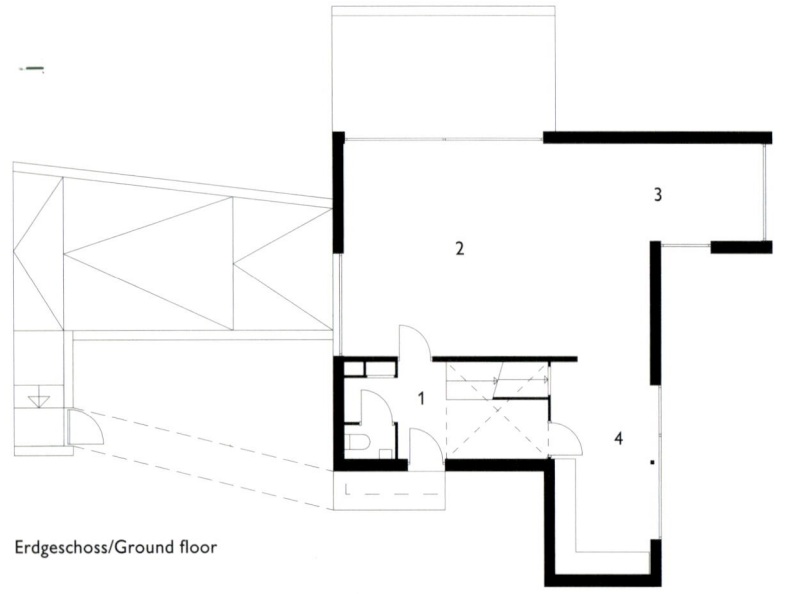

Erdgeschoss/Ground floor

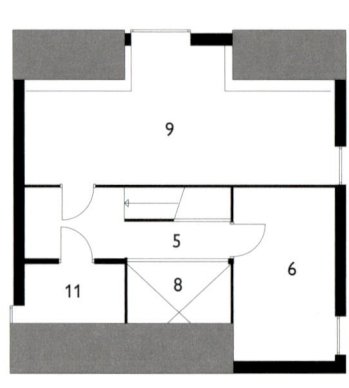

Zweites Geschoss/Second floor

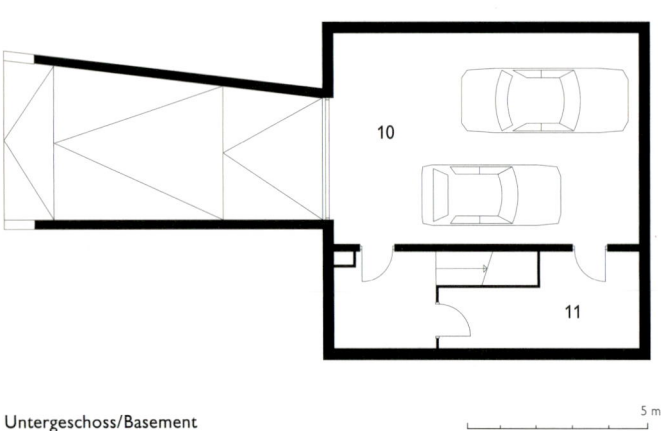

Untergeschoss/Basement

5 m

Erstes Geschoss/First floor

Grundschule Prinsehaghe, Den Haag

Prinsehaghe Primary School, The Hague

Entwurf/Design: 2001–2003
Ausführung/Construction: 2004–2005
Bauherrschaft/Client: Stichting Christelijk Onderwijs Haaglanden (SCOH)

Auszeichnung/Award:
Niederländischer Schulpreis 2006 ausgezeichnet durch das Ministerium für Bildung, Kultur und Wissenschaft/Dutch School Building Prize 2006 by the Ministry of Education, Culture and Science

Für einen geschlossenen Hof in der Innenstadt von Den Haag war eine Grundschule geplant, mit Einrichtungen zur Betreuung vor und nach dem Unterricht und einer Sporthalle. Der Hof ist aus den umliegenden Strassen über verschiedene Tore zwischen den Gebäuden erreichbar. Aufgrund der begrenzten Fläche des Grundstücks entschied man sich beim Entwurf für ein kompaktes, dreigeschossiges Gebäude. Eine durchgehende Treppe führt kaskadenförmig vom Eingang an der Südseite des Gebäudes bis hinauf ins zweite Obergeschoss. Die Klassenzimmer verteilen sich über alle drei Stockwerke. Neben dem Eingang befindet sich eine leicht abgesenkte Spielfläche; der zentrale Korridor kann bei Aufführungen oder Veranstaltungen als erhöhtes Podium genutzt werden. Über dem Eingang befindet sich ein grosser, multifunktionaler Arbeitsraum, über diesem die Sporthalle. Die Fassade und der Korridorbereich bilden das Tragwerk. Dadurch wurde es möglich, die einzelnen Klassenzimmer mit Faltwänden zu versehen und grosse Räume von bis zu 100 m² zu schaffen. Das Gebäude besitzt eine dauerhafte Fassade aus gelben, in Blockverband vermauerten Backsteinen und grosse Fenster mit bronzefarbenen Aluminiumrahmen. Der Eingangsbereich erhielt eine markante Verkleidung aus weissem Beton. Für die wartenden Eltern wurde eine überdachte Bank hinzugefügt. Im Inneren finden sich Fliesenböden und Holzvertäfelungen, die der ständigen Benutzung seitens der Kinder gut standhalten. Die Wände der Klassenzimmer sind farblich voneinander abgesetzt, was jedem Raum einen besonderen Akzent gibt, während die Wände der gemeinsamen Verkehrsflächen neutral weiss gehalten sind.

A primary school, with pre and after-school care, and a gym, were designed in a closed courtyard in The Hague city center. The courtyard is accessible from the surrounding streets through various gates between the houses. Due to the limited dimensions of the site a compact building was designed in three layers. The spatial axis of the building is provided by a continuous stairway which cascades from the second storey on the south side of the building all the way down to the entrance. The classrooms are divided over the three storeys. Next to the entrance there is a slightly sunken recreation room with the central corridor providing a raised platform for performances and events. A large multifunctional study area is situated above the entrance with the gym on top of that. The façade and corridor zone are the load-bearing structures, thereby making it possible to separate the classrooms with folding walls so that large spaces of up to 100 m² can be created. The building has a durable yellow brick façade laid in a decorative bond, with large windows and bronze-coloured aluminium frames. A white concrete surround accentuates the entrance. A bench with awning was added for waiting parents. For the interior, tiled floors and wood panelling were used that can withstand the wear and tear of everyday use by children. An individual colour was applied to one wall in each classroom. The walls of the generally frequented areas were painted in a neutral white.

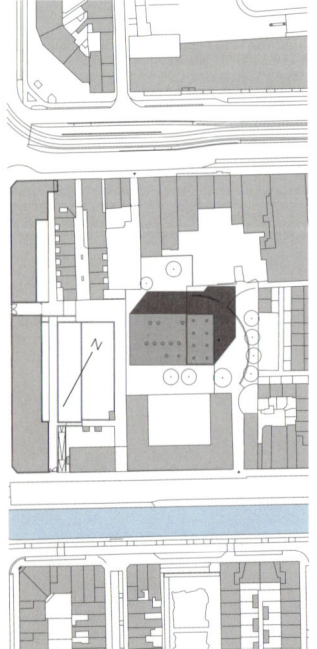

1 Haupteingang
2 Hausmeister
3 Zentraler Korridor mit Haupttreppe
4 Freizeitbereich
5 Klassenzimmer
6 nachschulische Betreuung
7 soziale Betreuung
8 multifunktionaler Arbeitsbereich
9 Lehrerzimmer
10 Verwaltung
11 Umkleideraum
12 Sporthalle
13 Schulhof

1 Main entrance
2 Porter
3 Central corridor with main stairs
4 Recreation room
5 Classroom
6 Afterschool
7 Social welfare
8 Multifunctional study area
9 Staff
10 Management
11 Dressing room
12 Gym
13 School yard

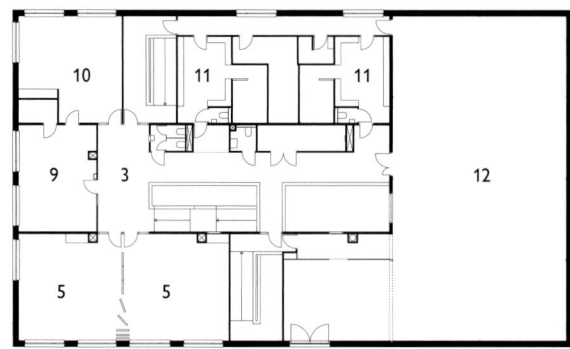

Zweites Geschoss/Second floor

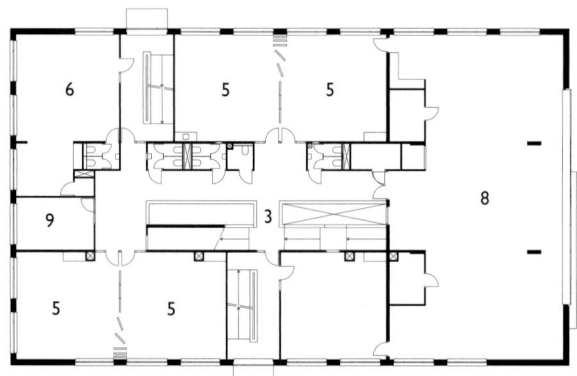

Erstes Geschoss/First floor

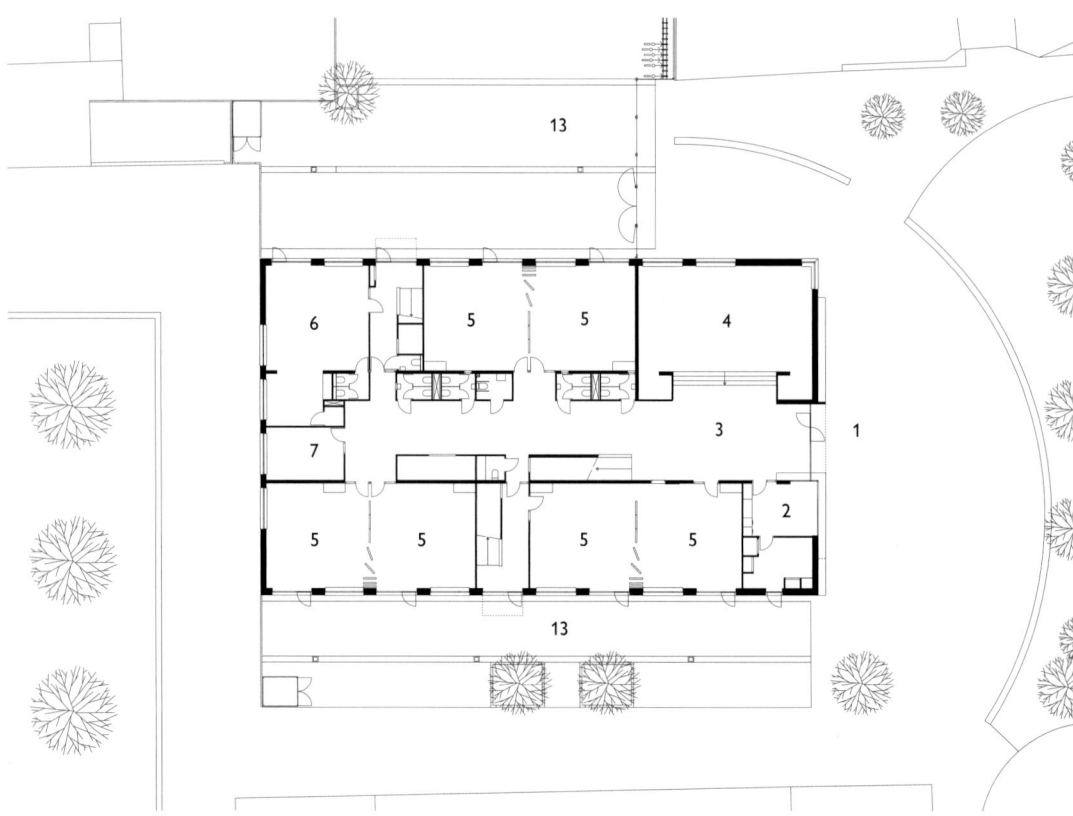

Erdgeschoss/Ground floor

10 m

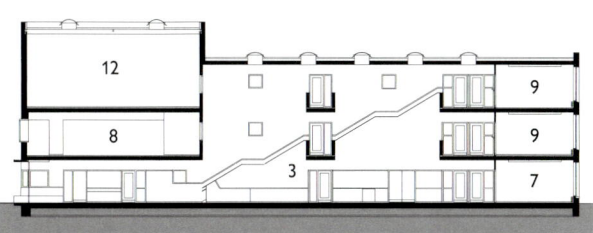

3

5

8

3

Wohnhochhaus Vermeertoren, Delft

Vermeer Tower, Delft

Entwurf/Design: 2001–2003
Ausführung/Construction: 2005–2007
Bauherrschaft/Client: Ceres Projecten

An der Kreuzung zwischen der Landesstrasse nach Rijswijk und dem Zugang zu einem Wohnviertel wurde ein 23-geschossiger Wohnturm errichtet. Der Turm markiert deutlich den Übergang in die Stadt. Um seine schlanke Masse zu gliedern und die Vertikalität zu steigern, wurden die drei Wohnungen pro Geschoss gegeneinander gestaffelt. Im obersten Geschoss wurde das Volumen des Penthouse so gestaltet, dass die Unterteilung des Hauptkörpers in der Höhenabstufung der drei Teile betont wird. In dem niedrigen Abschnitt sind Wohlfahrtseinrichtungen untergebracht, darunter ein Nachbarschaftszentrum, ein Jugendclub, ein Gesundheitszentrum und eine Apotheke, ausserdem eine Tiefgarage und ein Gartenhof. Die Fassaden, die bronzefarbene Fensterrahmen aus Aluminium haben und mit sandfarbenem Backstein verkleidet sind, präsentieren sich in Richtung der stark befahrenen Kreuzung relativ geschlossen, während sie sich nach Südwesten mit grossen Fenstern und verglasten Veranden öffnen. An sonnigen Tagen hebt sich der gelbe Turm strahlend von dem blauen Himmel ab – eine Farbkombination, die uns von dem berühmten Delfter Maler Vermeer vertraut ist, nach dem auch das Gebäude benannt ist. Von der Spitze des Gebäudes erblickt man eine heutige «Ansicht von Delft».

A 23-storey tower block was designed at the junction of the provincial road to Rijswijk and the entrance to a residential neighbourhood. The building represents a clear demarcation of the gateway to the city of Delft. The slender mass of the tower was articulated by staggering the three apartments per storey relative to one another, which reinforces the vertical effect. On the uppermost storey the volume of the penthouse underlines the division of the main structure into three parts, with one part staggered in height relative to another. The lower section houses welfare facilities such as a community centre, youth club, healthcare centre and pharmacy, together with underground parking and a garden courtyard. The façades, which are finished with sand-coloured brick and bronze-coloured aluminium window frames, are relatively closed in the direction of the busy junction and open up to the south-west side, with large windows and winter garden. On a sunny day the yellow tower stands out against the blue sky – the colours used by the famous Delft artist Vermeer, after whom the tower is named. From the top there is a splendid new 'View of Delft'.

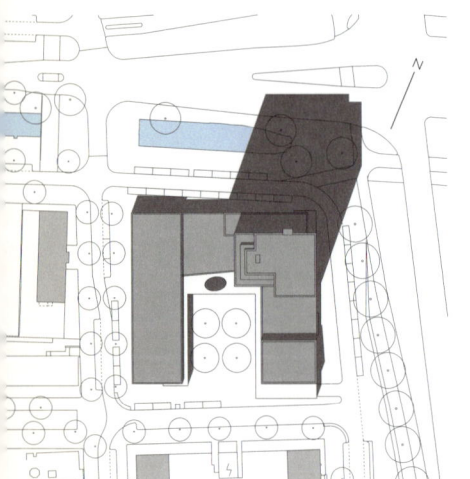

1 Eingang zu den Wohlfahrtseinrichtungen
2 zentrale Halle mit Haupttreppenhaus
3 Apotheke
4 Wohlfahrtseinrichtung
5 Gesundheitszentrum
6 Nachbarschaftszentrum
7 Arztpraxis
8 physiotherapeutische Praxis
9 Eingang zu den Wohnungen
10 Aufzugshalle
11 Wohnung
12 Tiefgarage
13 Fahrradaufbewahrung
14 Gartenhof

1 Entrance welfare facilities
2 Central hall with main stairs
3 Pharmacy
4 Welfare facility
5 Health care facility
6 Community centre
7 Medical practice
8 Physiotherapy practice
9 Entrance apartments
10 Elevator lobby
11 Apartment
12 Underground car park
13 Bicycle shed
14 Garden courtyard

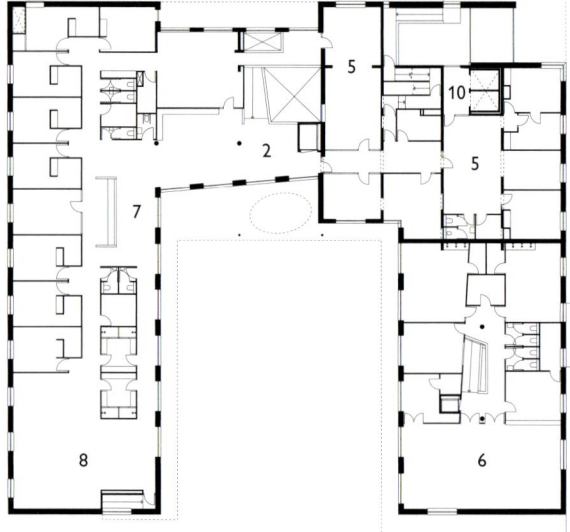

Erstes Geschoss/First floor

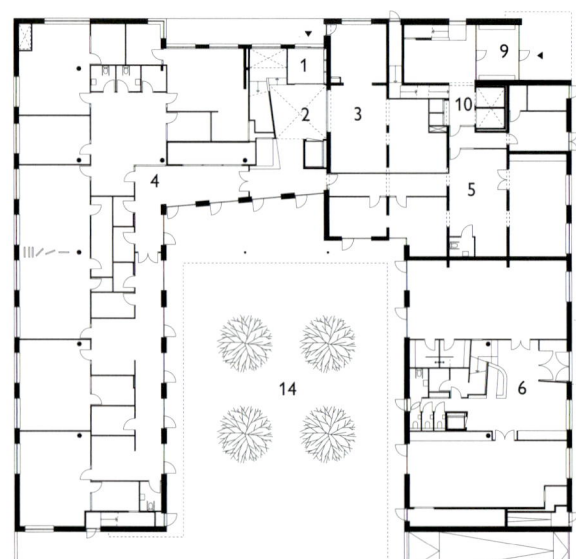

Erdgeschoss/Ground floor

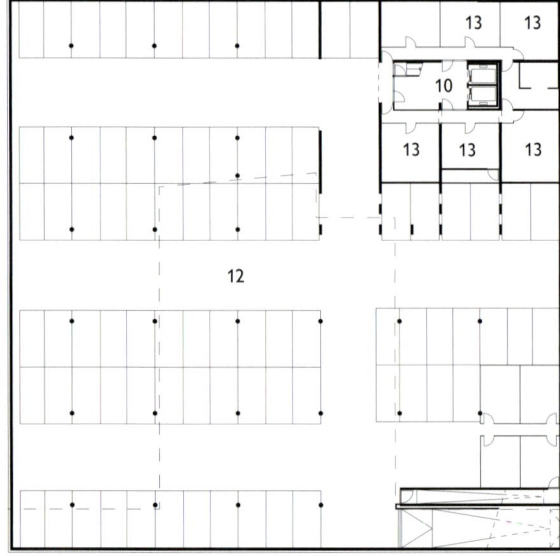

10 m

Untergeschoss/Basement

2.–22. Standardgeschoss/2nd–22nd standard floor   23. Geschoss/23rd floor   24. Dachgeschoss/24th penthouse floor

6

6

7

4

7

Wohnanlage Het Funen, Amsterdam

Het Funen Residential Estate, Amsterdam

Entwurf/Design: 1999–2000
Ausführung/Construction: 2005–2007
Bauherrschaft/Client: Heijmans IBC
Vastgoed bv

Auszeichnung/Award: Nominierung
für den Architekturpreis Amsterdam
2009/Nomination, Amsterdam
Architecture Prize 2009

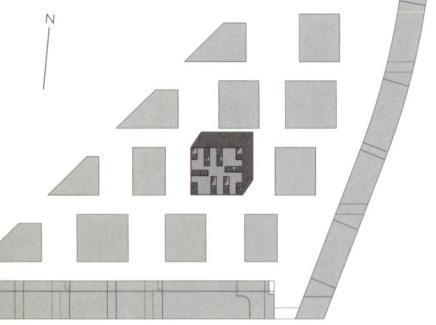

Auf einem ehemaligen Gewerbegelände in Amsterdam-Oost wurden zehn dreigeschossige Wohnungen in Form von aneinandergesetzten Häusern in einem introvertierten Block untergebracht. Da dieser eng von anderen Gebäuden umringt ist, erhielt jedes Haus einen eigenen, über alle drei Ebenen gehenden Innenhof. In dem Block gibt es drei Grundtypen: das Eckhaus, das breite und das langgestreckte Haus. Die Wohnungen umgeben den jeweiligen Innenhof, auf den man aus den oberen Geschossen hinabblickt. Gleichzeitig schafft der Hof Beziehungen zwischen den verschiedenen Innenräumen und der Aussenwelt. Die Treppen wurden so angelegt, dass sie eine direkte Verbindung vom Erdgeschoss zur Dachterrasse im zweiten Obergeschoss herstellen.

Die mit Betonfertigteilen verkleideten Fassaden haben vertikale Fensteröffnungen. Stahlseile an der Fassade erlauben eine Begrünung derselben. Die Dachflächen sind mit Moos bepflanzt. So erscheinen die einzelnen Gebäudeteile wie von einer grünen Hülle umfangen. Die Räume im Inneren dieser Hülle erhalten über den Innenhof überraschend viel Tageslicht.

Ten three-storey apartments were built in the form of terraced houses on a former industrial estate in Amsterdam-Oosten within an introverted block development. Because the houses are close to other built structures in the vicinity, each home was given its own patio on all three levels. The block has three basic types: a corner house, a wide terraced house and a longer type. The apartments surround each courtyard, upon which the upper storeys look down. This inner courtyard creates relationships between the various interior spaces and the outside world. The stairs were placed to gives direct access from the ground floor to a roof terrace on the second floor.

The façades, finished in prefabricated concrete, have vertical window frames. Steel wires over the façade enable greenery to be trained upwards. The roofs are also covered with moss. The vegetation creates a green shell around the building.

1 Patio
2 Stauraum
3 Eingangsbereich
4 Schlafzimmer
5 Leerraum
6 Küche
7 Wohnzimmer
8 Terrasse
9 Arbeitszimmer

1 Patio
2 Storage
3 Hall
4 Bedroom
5 Void
6 Kitchen
7 Livingroom
8 Terrace
9 Study

Zweites Geschoss/Second floor

Erstes Geschoss/First floor

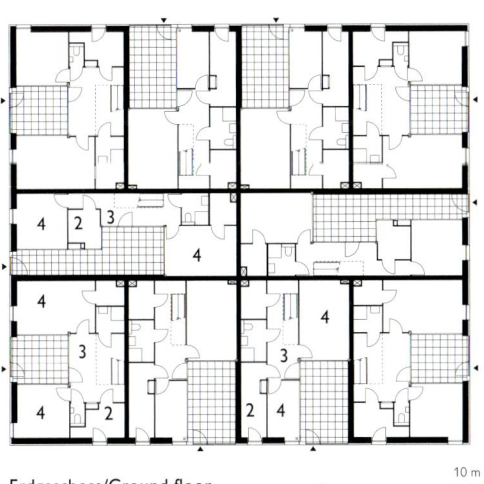

Erdgeschoss/Ground floor

10 m

Wohnüberbauung Le Medi Rotterdam

Le Medi Residential Building, Rotterdam

Entwurf/Design: 2004–2006
Ausführung/Construction: 2007–2008
Bauherrschaft/Client: Com-Wonen,
Era Bouw, Woonbron

Auszeichnungen/Awards: Architektur-
preis Rotterdam 2009/Rotterdam
Architecture Prize 2009;
Architekturpreis Farbe 2011/Dutch
Colour Award 2011 (Kleur Buiten Prijs
2011)

Auf Initiative eines Geschäftsmanns marokkanischer Herkunft wurde in einem bestehenden Rotterdamer Wohnviertel ein neues städtisches Quartier mit mediterranen Merkmalen entwickelt. Die neue Gestaltung soll den Austausch kultureller Werte befördern helfen und der Gesamtanlage eine starke eigene Identität verleihen. Die Bebauung ist um einen rechteckigen Platz angeordnet, der über ein imposantes Tor und drei Wohnstrassen erreichbar ist. Das Quartier ist autofreie Zone. Garagen befinden sich unter den Sonnenterrassen der Häuser. Die meisten Wohnhäuser sind dreigeschossig. Im ersten Obergeschoss befindet sich das Wohnzimmer, von dem aus man einen Zugang zu der Sonnenterrasse über der Garage hat. Den Bewohnern steht es frei, den Häusern ein weiteres Stockwerk oder einen Anbau über der Garage hinzuzufügen. Die Aussenseiten des Blocks wurden als eine geschlossene Stadtmauer aus lehmfarbenem Backstein in verschiedenen Verbänden und mit dekorativen Umrahmungen der Tür- und Fensteröffnungen aus weissem Naturstein entworfen. Vier Tore führen zu den Wohnstrassen, in denen sich die Häuser mit einer getünchten Backsteinfassade präsentieren. Jedes Haus erhielt eine eigene Farbe, ausgewählt aus einem festgelegten Farbschema. Die Strassen sind mit Backsteinen gepflastert. Auf dem Platz mit seinem mediterran gestalteten Springbrunnen laden Bänke unter Akazienbäumen zum Sitzen ein. Das Projekt stärkt das Zusammengehörigkeitsgefühl der Einwohner, die einen unterschiedlichen ethnischen Hintergrund haben.

On the initiative of a businessman of Moroccan origin, a new urban planning concept with Mediterranean features was developed in an existing residential district of Rotterdam, with the aim of exchanging cultural values and creating a strong local identity. The block is arranged around a square which can be entered through an imposing gateway and from three residential streets. The entire block is car free. Cars can be parked under the sun terraces of the houses. Most of the homes have three storeys with the living room on the first floor giving access to the outdoor space over the garage. Residents can add an extra floor or build an extension on top of the garage. The outer perimeter of the block was designed as an enclosing city wall in a varied brickwork bond pattern using clay coloured bricks with decorative white stone surrounds. Four gates provide access to the streets on which every house has a painted brick façade in its own colour within a set colour scheme. The streets have brick paving. The square has benches set among the Acacia trees and includes a Mediterranean style fountain. The project has led to a greater sense of solidarity among the residents of differing ethnic backgrounds.

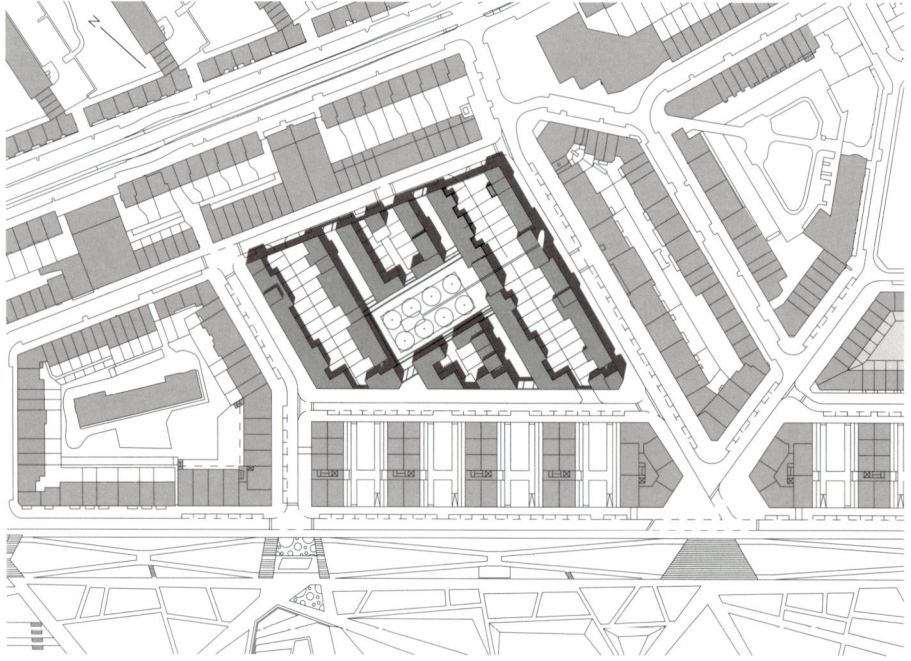

1 Haupttor
2 Eingang zur Wohnstrasse
3 Zentraler Platz mit Springbrunnen
4 Garten
5 Eingang Parkhaus
6 Garage
7 Sonnenterrasse

1 Main gateway
2 Entrance residential street
3 Central square with fountain
4 Garden
5 Entrance parking
6 Car park
7 Sun terrace

20 m

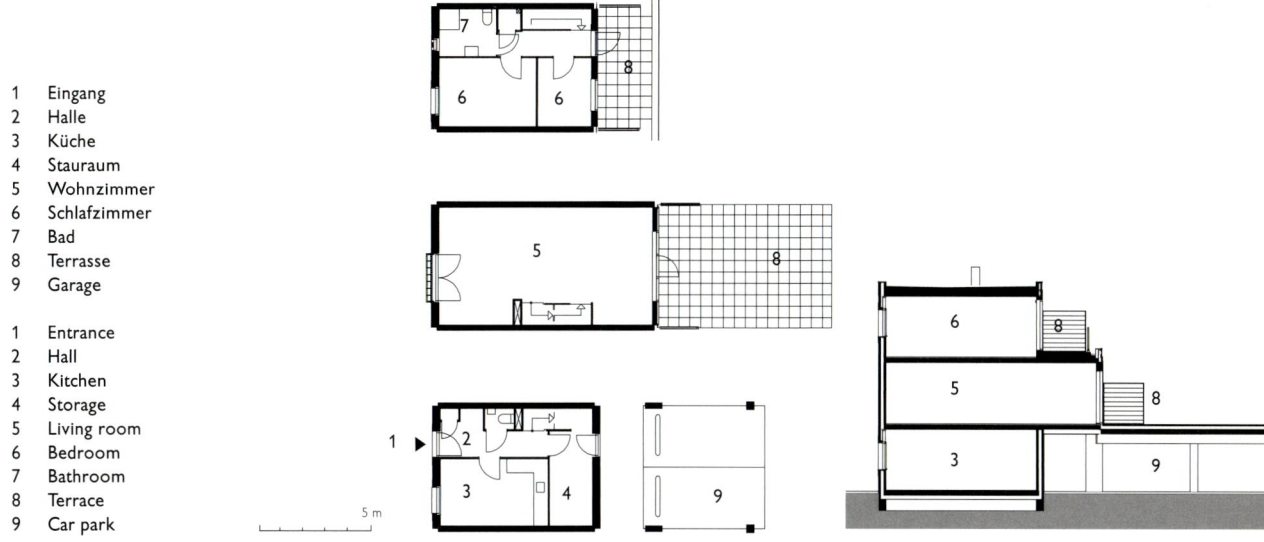

1	Eingang
2	Halle
3	Küche
4	Stauraum
5	Wohnzimmer
6	Schlafzimmer
7	Bad
8	Terrasse
9	Garage

1	Entrance
2	Hall
3	Kitchen
4	Storage
5	Living room
6	Bedroom
7	Bathroom
8	Terrace
9	Car park

5 m

47

Wohnkomplex Bos en Lommer, Amsterdam

Bos en Lommer Residential Development, Amsterdam

Entwurf/Design: 2004–2006
Ausführung/Construction: 2006–2008
Bauherrschaft/Client: Hillen en Roosen
Projectontwikkeling

Auszeichnung/Award: Architekturpreis
2009/Zuiderkerk Prize 2009

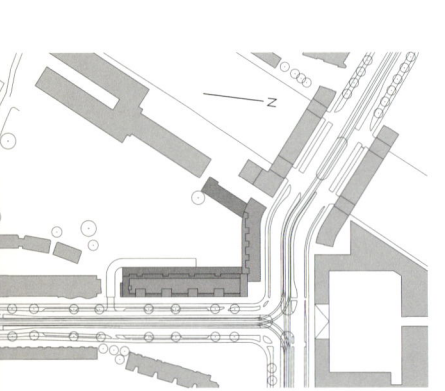

Dieser städtische Block ist Teil eines Stadterneuerungsprojekts, mit dessen Hilfe das alte Zentrum eines Ortsteils revitalisiert wird. Das Projekt verbindet ein Quartier, das in den 1920er und 1930er Jahren im Stil der Amsterdamer Architekturschule gebaut wurde, mit einer Stadterweiterung aus der Zeit nach dem Zweiten Weltkrieg. Der neue Wohnblock umfasst drei Flügel mit jeweils verschiedenen Wohnungstypen und eine Tiefgarage. Am Hoofdweg an der Ostseite liegen Apartmentblocks mit drei Apartments pro Aufgang sowie einem Gesundheitszentrum und einer Polizeiwache im Erdgeschoss. Der Block im Norden wurde aufgestelzt, um Zugang zu einem Park zu ermöglichen. Die Eingänge zu den einzelnen Wohnungen liegen längs eines Gangs. Die gekurvte Fassade dieses Blocks folgt dem Schwenk des Bos en Lommerwegs. An der Westseite des Komplexes gibt es Wohnungen für junge Menschen. Die Fassaden präsentieren sich mit ockerfarbenem Backstein und weissen Fensterrahmen aus Holz. Bei den strassenseitigen Fassaden der Apartmentblocks finden sich in den dekorativen Elementen und in der besonderen Detaillierung der Fensterrahmen Anklänge an die Amsterdamer Schule. Die zum Park führenden Fassaden weisen zwischen den Backsteinlagen horizontale weisse Betonbänder auf, die an die Architektur des Wiederaufbaus nach dem Zweiten Weltkrieg anknüpfen.

This urban block forms part of a city redevelopment project intended to revitalize an old district centre. The project links an area built in the 1920s and '30s in the Amsterdam School style of architecture with a post-war city expansion development. The residential block consists of an underground garage and has three wings, each providing different types of housing. Along Hoofdweg on the east side there are apartment blocks with an entrance hall, each as well as three apartments per floor, along with a healthcare centre and a police station on the ground floor. The northern block is raised on stilts to provide access to a park and has a corridor for accessing the apartments. The curved façade of the block follows the bend of the road Bos en Lommerweg. The west side of the complex provides housing for young people. The façades have ochre-coloured brickwork with white wooden window frames. The façades on the street side of the apartment blocks exhibit features of the Amsterdam School in terms of the decorative elements and the particular detailing of the window frames. Bands of concrete in between sections of brick have been used for the façades on the park side, thereby creating a link with the architecture of the post-war reconstruction period.

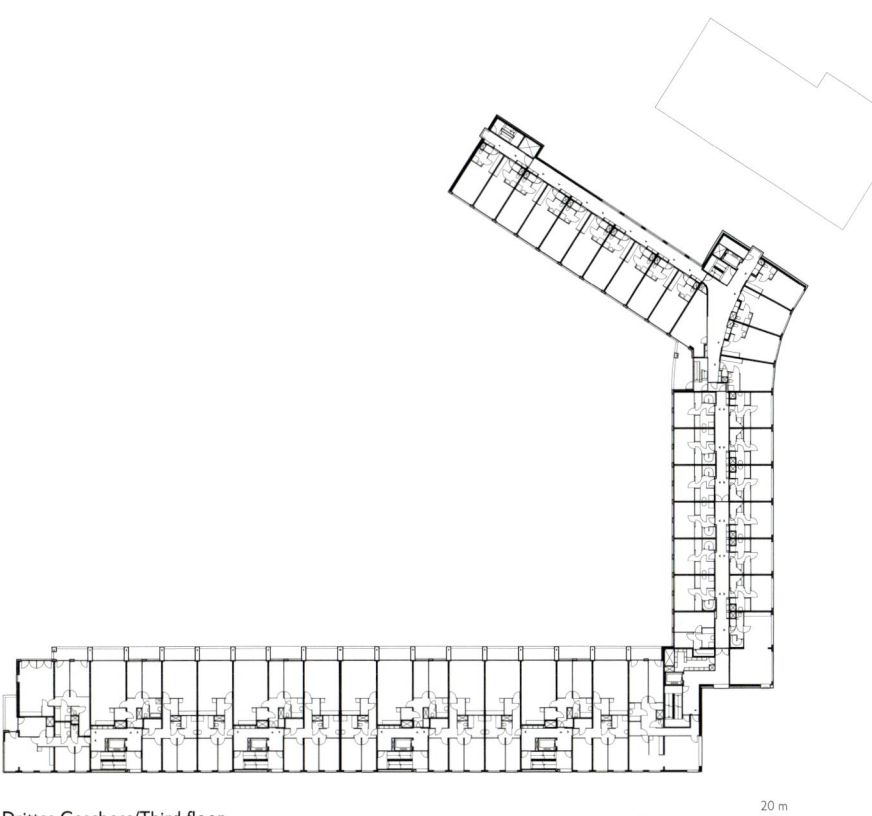

Drittes Geschoss/Third floor

20 m

Überbauung Andreas
Ensemble, Amsterdam

Urban Building Andreas
Ensemble, Amsterdam

Entwurf/Design: 2004–2006
Ausführung/Construction: 2006–2011
Bauherrschaft/Client: Proper Stok
Ontwikkelaars, De Alliantie
Projectontwikkeling

Auszeichnungen/Awards:
Nominierung Architekturpreis
Amsterdam 2012/Nomination,
Amsterdam Architecture Prize 2012;
Nominierung Bauwerk des Jahres
2012 – Niederländische
Architektenkammer/Nomination, BNA
Building of the Year 2012

Das ehemalige Gelände des Andreas Ziekenhuis Hospitals liegt in einem durchgrünten Gebiet südlich des städtischen Lelylaan und östlich der Ringstrasse A10. Es verbindet die geschlossen bebaute, von H. P. Berlage geplante Stadterweiterung aus der Vorkriegszeit mit der offeneren Bebauung der Westelijke Tuinsteden (westlichen Gartenstädte), die in der Nachkriegszeit von C. van Eesteren entworfen wurden. Das neue Projekt versucht, mit einem offenen Grossblock an die Qualitäten eben dieser Bebauungen anzuknüpfen. Der Block wurde als ein kohärentes Ensemble von Gebäuden entworfen, die durch gleiche Farben und Baumaterialien miteinander verbunden sind. Dank der offenen Anlage schliessen die gemeinsamen, begrünten Höfe bruchlos an den südlich gelegenen Park an. Neben einer grossen Zahl von Wohnungen liessen sich auf dem zentral gelegenen Areal diverse Funktionen unterbringen, darunter ein Hotel, ein Kinderhort, eine Bar sowie diverse Läden. Die Wohngebäude wurden in Zusammenarbeit mit dem Architekten Tony Fretton entworfen. Sie sind in einzelne, viergeschossige Wohnhäuser mit jeweils eigenem Eingang untergliedert. Im Norden und Westen bilden die Wohngebäude eine geschlossene Wand, an den anderen Seiten präsentieren sie sich als frei stehende Häuser. Zwischen den Blocks wurden über der Tiefgarage unterschiedlich bepflanzte Grünflächen geschaffen. Unter Ausnutzung der vorhandenen Höhendifferenz wurden die gartenähnlichen Flächen auf zwei Niveaus angelegt, die durch Treppen miteinander verbunden sind. Die Fassaden sind mit sandfarbenem Backstein verkleidet und haben bronzefarbene Fensterrahmen aus Aluminium. Der Materialeinsatz variiert pro Fassade. Die Abmessungen der Fensterrahmen, Balustraden, Geländer, Wandflächen und Treppen beruhen auf einem System festgelegter Verhältnisgrössen, die von den Massen eines Backsteins abgeleitet sind.

The site of the former Andreas Ziekenhuis hospital lies in a greenbelt area to the south of the urban Lelylaan and east of the A10 ring road. It links the block structures of the pre-war city expansion development designed by H.P. Berlage and the more open planning of the post-war Westelijke Tuinsteden (western garden cities) laid out by C. van Eesteren. The plan aimed to unify the qualities of these two approaches through an open super block. The super block was designed as a coherent ensemble of buildings connected to one another through the use of colour and materials. The open layout of the block connects the communal green courtyards with a park on the south side. Besides the large number of homes provided, various functions in the area could be brought together at this central location, such as a hotel, a crèche, a bar and shops. The residential buildings were designed together with the architect Tony Fretton and consist of four-storey apartment blocks with their own entrance halls. On the north and west sides the apartment buildings have been joined to create a city wall. On the other side they stand as distinct separate structures. Between the blocks a series of varied communal gardens has been laid out on top of the underground car park. Making use of an existing height difference, the gardens were laid out on two levels linked by steps. The façades have been finished in sand-coloured brick combined with bronze-coloured aluminium window frames. Variation was introduced into each façade through the materials used. The proportions for the window frames, balustrades, guardrails, wall surfaces and steps were selected on the basis of a system of fixed ratios derived from the size of a brick.

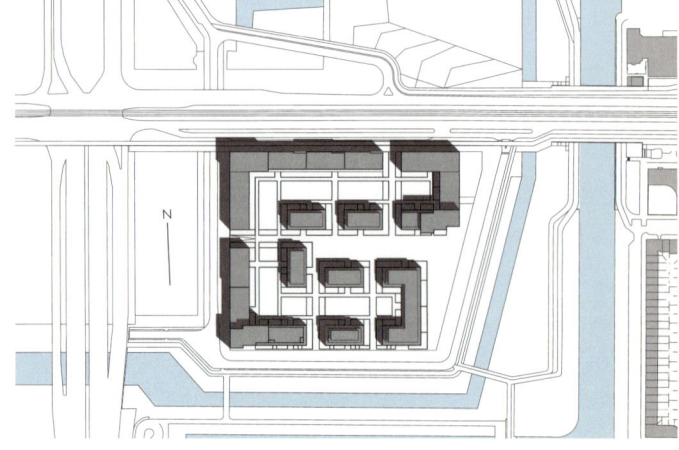

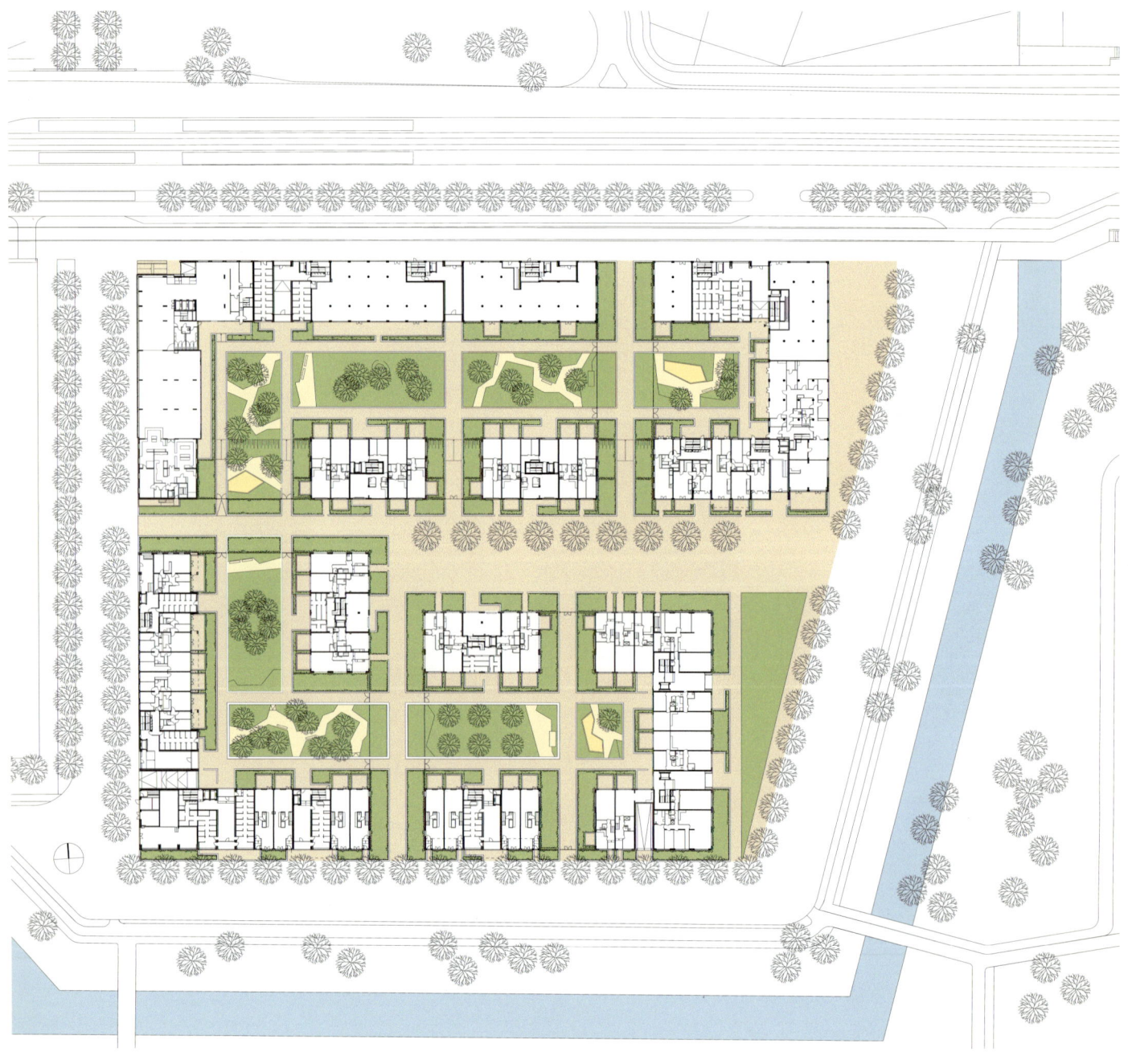

40 m

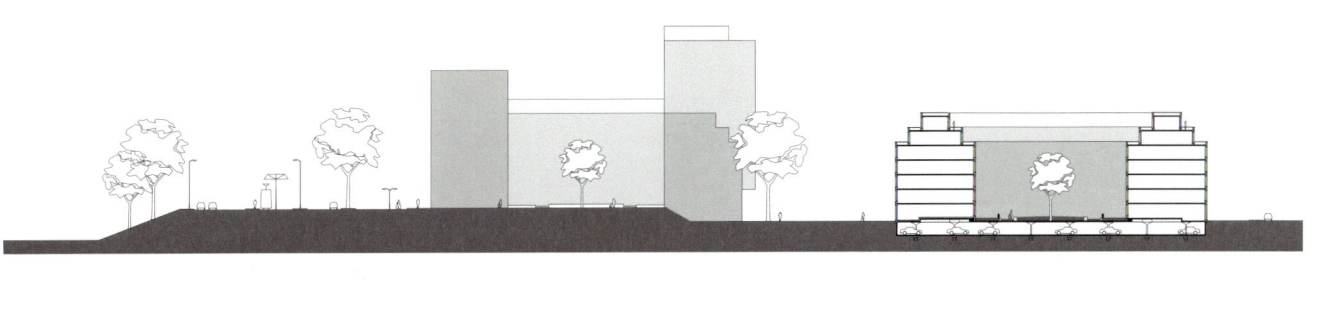

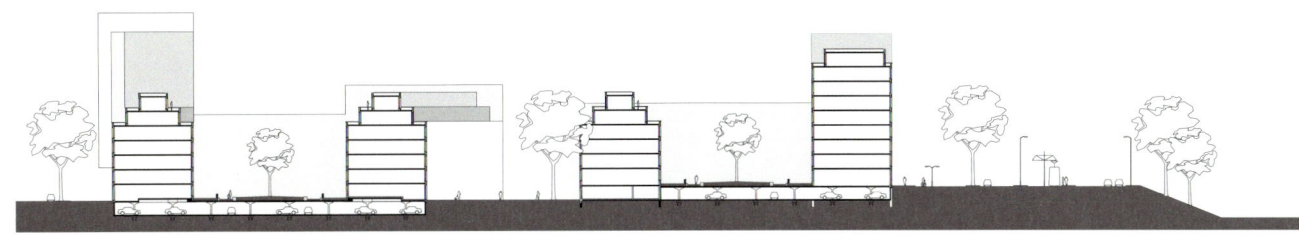

54

Viertes Geschoss/4th floor

Zwölftes Geschoss/12th floor

10 m

Werkverzeichnis/List of Works
Auswahl Bauten, Projekte und Wettbewerbe/Selection of Buildings, Projects and Competitions

1983		Louwse Poort Den Bosch, 7 apartments and commercial space
1987		Boschdijk Eindhoven, 40 student apartments
	1	Jacob Marisstraat The Hague, 92 houses with 2 car parks
1988		Urban Villa *Woningbouwfestival* The Hague
1989		Urban design Tussenwater Hoogvliet Rotterdam
		Corpus den Hoorn Groningen, 134 houses
		Doedijnstraat The Hague, 238 houses with car park (design Alvaro Siza)
1990		Museum of Scotland Edinburgh, design competition
1991		Parallelweg The Hague, 316 houses with car park
1992		Bilderdijkstraat The Hague, 60 student apartments
		Laakhaven The Hague, 108 houses, commercial space and car park
		Vijverkwartier Almere, 152 houses
1993		Java-eiland Amsterdam, 149 houses and car park
1994		Weerdjesstraat Arnhem, 71 houses and commercial space
1995		Raaks Haarlem, 38 houses, commercial space and car park
		Adriaan Mulderstraat Utrecht, 40 apartments and car park
		Slachthuisterrein Hilversum, 80 houses with car park
1996		Loevesteinlaan The Hague, 50 houses with car park
1997		Erasmusweg The Hague, 69 houses, offices and car park
	2	Doelenterrein Delft, 23 houses
		Laakhaven The Hague, 4 towers with 265 apartments
		2nd Harbour Scheveningen, 40 apartments, offices and car park
		Vliegerheem The Hague, 163 houses, commercial space and car park

1

2

3

4

5

6

7

8

9

10

11

2009		Community school De Amstelmeer Amsterdam
		CZAN Amsterdam, 112 houses, commercial space and parking
2010		RIZ-Bouw IJsselstein, industrial building and offices
		Primary school Reet-Niel, Belgium
		De Slinger Houten, urban design in cooperation with Rein Geurtsen & Partners
		Schenkweg The Hague, 67 student houses
		Visserijplein Rotterdam, urban design
2011	**15**	Memorial Park 2014–2018, West Flanders Belgium, memorial WWI
		Bridges in Tuindorp Rotterdam, 4 slow road bridges
		Sports facility Motorstraat Rotterdam
		Wijnhaven District The Hague, reallocating former ministries
2012		SARP offices Gezondheidspark Dordrecht, Sanquin Blood Supply, clinic and offices
		Ringspoorzone Kolenkit Amsterdam, 113 houses and car park
		Kooiplein Leiden, 77 houses, commercial space and car park
		Orthen Links Den Bosch, 50 apartments
		Waldorpstraat The Hague, 80 apartments
		VTI Roeselare, Belgium, educational building
		HBOV St. Michiels, Belgium, educational building
		GVKS Virgo Maria Merksem, Belgium, primary school and nursery school
		VBS De Vlinder Baarle-Hertog Belgium, primary school and nursery school
		GVBS De Wijngaard Laakdal, Belgium, primary school and nursery school
2013		Community school De Oase Utrecht

12

13

14

15

Jeroen Geurst

1960	geboren in Delft
1978–1986	Diplomabschluss in Architektur an der Technischen Universität in Delft
1984	Gründung von Geurst & Schulze Architecten in Den Haag
1990–	Dozent an der Akademie für Architektur in Amsterdam
1993–1995	Dozent an der Akademie für Architektur in Arnhem
1995–1998	Mitglied des Architektur Plattform Wils & Co in Den Haag
1995–1999	Teilzeit Leiter der Abteilung Architektur, Staatliches Amt für Bauten
1997–2003	Supervisor Singels Ypenburg Den Haag
1999–2002	Mitglied und Vorsitzender des Gestaltungsbeirats Breda
2000–	Supervisor Transvaal Den Haag
2003–2009	Mitglied des Gestaltungsbeirats Rotterdam
2003–	Supervisor Punt- Schippers Bezirk Rotterdam
2004–	Supervisor Campus Overhoeks Amsterdam
2005	Mitglied Niederländischer Rat für Bau- und Konstruktionsreformen
2010–2011	Gastkritiker an der Akademie für Architektur in Rotterdam
2010–	Supervisor Lloydpier Rotterdam
2011–	Dozent an der Akademie für Architektur in Arnhem
2013	Gastkritiker an der Universität in Dundee
2013–	Dozent an der Akademie für Architektur in Rotterdam

1960	Born in Delft
1978–1986	Diploma Delft University of Technology, Faculty of Architecture
1984	Founded Geurst & Schulze Architecten
1990–	Present tutor at the Academy of Architecture Amsterdam
1993–1995	Tutor at the Academy of Architecture Arnhem
1995–1998	Member of Wils & Co, foundation for architecture The Hague
1995–1999	Part-time Head of Department of Architecture at the Government Buildings Agency
1997–2003	Supervisor Singels Ypenburg The Hague
1999–2002	Member and chairman of the Breda Planning Committee
2000–	Present supervisor Transvaal The Hague
2003–2009	Member of Rotterdam Planning Committee
2003–	Present supervisor Punt- Schippers District Rotterdam
2004–	Present supervisor Campus Overhoeks Amsterdam
2005	Member of Dutch Council for Reform in Building and Construction
2010–2011	'Visiting critic' at the Rotterdam Academy of Architecture
2010–	Present supervisor Lloydpier Rotterdam
2011	Tutor at the Academy of Architecture Arnhem
2013	'Visiting critic' at the University of Dundee, School of Environment
2013–	Present tutor at the Rotterdam Academy of Architecture

Publikationen/Publications

1983	Exhibition with catalogue "L.C. van der Vlugt, architect 1894–1936" in cooperation with Joris Molenaar
1990	Wiederhall, essay 'the house of C.H. van der Leeuw'
1992	GA, Global Architecture Japan, essay 'The Van Nelle Factory'
2002	SKRO 04-2002, essay Cemeteries WWI
2005	Western Front Association The Netherlands, essay 'the Great War'
2007	De Architect 2007/1, 'design and research of Geurst & Schulze architects'
2007	OASE #72, essay 'back to school'
2010	'Cemeteries of the Great War by Sir Edwin Lutyens', 010 Publishers
2011	Vlaamse Vereniging Ruimte en Planning: "Groene Kathedralen in de Westhoek" Baksteen nr. 60 "Tektoniek. De maat en de orde van de gebakken steen"

Rens Schulze	1960	geboren in Schiedam
	1978–1986	Diplomabschluss in Architektur an der Technischen Universität in Delft
	1984	Gründung von Geurst & Schulze Architecten in Den Haag
	1992–1993	Dozent an der Universität für Technologie in Delft
	1994–1996	Dozent an der Akademie für Architektur in Amsterdam
	1995–2001	Dozent an der Akademie für Architektur in Tilburg
	1997–2001	Mitglied des Gestaltungsbeirats Amsterdam
	1997–2001	Dozent an der Akademie für Architektur in Rotterdam
	2004–2005	Dozent an der Technischen Universität in Delft
	2006–2012	Vorsitzender des Gestaltungsbeirats Delft
	seit 2008	Präsident der Gesellschaft Architectura et Amicitia in Amsterdam
	seit 2009	Vorsitzender Qualitätsteam 'Spoorzone' in Delft
	1960	Born in Schiedam
	1978–1986	Diploma Delft University of Technology, Faculty of Architecture
	1984	Founded Geurst & Schulze Architecten
	1992–1993	Tutor at Delft University of Technology
	1994–1996	Tutor at the Academy of Architecture Amsterdam
	1995–2001	Tutor at the Academy of Architecture Tilburg
	1997–2001	Member of the Amsterdam Planning Committee
	1997–2001	Tutor at the Rotterdam Academy of Architecture
	2004–2005	Tutor at Delft University of Technology
	2006–2012	Chairman of the Delft Planning Committee
	2008–	Present chairman of Architectura et Amicitia in Amsterdam
	2009–	Present chairman of the Quality team 'Spoorzone' in Delft

Ausstellungen/Auszeichnungen Exhibitions/Awards	1989	Biënnale Young Dutch Architects, HAL Rotterdam
	1997	"Berlagevlag" The Hague City Council Prize
	2000	"Inside Out", ABC-Haarlem Centre of Architecture
	2003	Nomination Mies van der Rohe Award
		"Stadsprijs" The Hague City Council Prize
	2004	Mobile urbanism "In de Tussentijd", Stroom The Hague
	2005	"United Colors of NL", ABC-Haarlem Centre of Architecture
		"NL Trots?", ABC-Haarlem Centre of Architecture
	2006	Dutch School Building Award
		"United Colors of NL", Aorta-Utrecht Centre of Architecture
		"Primary School Prinsehaghe The Hague", Stroom The Hague
	2007	Rotterdam Architecture Prize
	2008	Honorable Mention Rotterdam Architecture Prize
	2009	Honorable mention Building Business Golden Green Awards
		Nomination Amsterdam Architecture Prize
		Amsterdam Zuiderkerk Prize
		Rotterdam Architecture Prize
	2011	"Kleur Buiten Prijs" Colour Award
	2012	Nomination Rotterdam Architecture Prize
		Nomination Amsterdam Architecture Prize
		Nomination BNA Building of the Year
	2013	Nomination Amsterdam Architecture Prize

MitarbeiterInnen/Collaborators — Frans Bochanen, Marc-Jan Boerman, Joop Bolster, Jurriën van Duijkeren, Paul van Duijvenbode, Linda van Eijk-Cornelis, Martina van Ess, Jan de Haan, Remco van Kampen, Peter Keller, Elco van de Kreke, Wendy Kroon, Valerie Koppelle, David Lesterhuis, Klaas van Olphen, Cissy Strengers-Snijders, Sjors Verhaar, Robin van de Ven, Xander Verburg, Nils van der Waal, Christiane Wirth

Bibliografie/Bibliography

1983	I. Salomons: Prijsvraag 's-Hertogenbosch. In: Forum 1983-3, Amsterdam
1985	Bossche prijsvraagontwerpen worden gebouwd. In: AB Architectuur Bouwen nr. 4, Rijswijk
1987	T. Maas: Succesvolle prijsvraag Den Bosch voltooid. In: AB Architectuur Bouwen nr. 1, Rijswijk
	Stadsvernieuwende woningbouw te 's Hertogenbosch. In: Bouw nr. 9, The Hague
	D. Postel: Lof der eenvoud. In: De Architect nr. 9, The Hague
1989	Biennale Jonge Nederlandse Architecten. Edition: B. Colenbrander, NAi Rotterdam
	L. Melis: Follies als vrijblijvende ontwerpopgave. In: De Architect 1, The Hague
1990	J. Verwijnen: Neues aus den Niederlande. In: Werk Bauen + Wohnen 1/2/1990, St. Gallen
1991	W. Looise/M. Klaren: Siza naar de kroon gestoken. In: De Architect nr. 9, The Hague
1992	C. Zwinkels: Kubussen, Urban villa van Geurst & Schulze. In: De Architect nr. 9, The Hague
	Architecture in the Netherlands, Yearbook 1991–1992. Amsterdam: NAi Publisher
1993	J. van Geest: Een heldere stadsrand, sociale woningbouw langs het Hoornse Meer, Groningen
1994	R. Ridderhof: Detachement and involvement, Berlage Prize. Edited by Dr. H.P. Berlage Foundation
	Architecture in the Netherlands, Yearbook 1993–1994. Amsterdam: NAi publisher
	J. Duursma: Woningbouw in Groningen 1978–1993. Rotterdam: 010 Publishers
1995	R. Ridderhof: Siedlung in Schilderswijk. In: Bauwelt nr. 13, Berlin
	M. Pflug/M.A. Visser: Stedebouw en kleur. Bussum: Thoth Publishers
1996	A. Oosterman: Housing in the Netherlands. Rotterdam: NAi Publishers
1997	H. van Dijk: Colour as Ambition. In: Archis nr. 12, Rotterdam
1998	W. Stamm-Teske: Preiswerter Wohnungbau in den Niederlande. Düsseldorf: Verlag Bau + Technik
1999	A. Mostaedi: Residential Complexes. 17 Residential houses De Aker Amsterdam. Barcelona: Links

2000	V. Freijser: Stad in vorm. Rotterdam: 010 Publishers
	Sun and Architecture. Edited by Solar Energy Programmes of Novem, Utrecht
2001	R. van Gool: Das Niederländische Reihenhaus. Serie und Vielvalt. Stuttgart/München: DVA
	K. Havik: Sober en Humaan. In: De Architect juni 2001, The Hague
2002	C. Masotti: Construire sostenibile l'Europa. Florence: Alinea
	A. Worthman: Passage through no-man's land. In Archis nr. 1, Amsterdam
	Th. Dupas: Centre pour demandeurs d'asile, Ter Appel Pay Bas. In : L'Architecure d'Aujourd'hui nr. 340/mai-juin, Paris
	Architecture in the Netherlands, Yearbook 2001–2002. Rotterdam: NAi publishers
	R. van Gool: Stadtvilla, Stadthaus, Parkhaus. In: Werk, Bauen + Wohnen nr. 10, Zürich
2003	H. van der Heijden: Innovatie van het bouwblok. In: De Architect mei 2003, The Hague
2004	H. Ibbelings: Onmoderne Architectuur. Rotterdam: NAi Publishers
2006	D. van Hoogstraten: De Haagse School. Rotterdam: NAi Publishers
2007	C. Rattray: Rationalist Traces. In: AD architectural design Vol. 77. London: John Wiley & Son
	R. Brouwers: Thema: woonwijk als leerschool. In: Stadscahiers nr. 2. Haarlem: Trancity
	F. R. Castelli: Scuola elementare en L'Aia Olanda. In: L'Industria delle Costruzioni nr. 398, Rome
2008	T. Verstegen: Een traditie van Verandering. Rotterdam: NAi Publishers/Staro
	H. van de Heijden: Hoog boven de Naoorlogse stad. In: De Architect juli-augustus 2008, The Hague: Sdu Publishers
	A. Aarsen: Een nieuw zicht op Delft. In: Stadcahiers 2008–2009. Haarlem: SUN Trancity
	Le Medi. Edited by Com Wonen, Era Bouw, Woonbron, Rotterdam
2009	M. Cousins: Design Quality in New Housing. Abingdon UK: Taylor & Francis Group
	Architecture in the Netherlands, Yearbook 2008–2009. Rotterdam: NAi Publishers
	H. van de Heijden: Act of Mediation. In: BD Building Design April 3-2009, London
	P. Groenendijk: Le Medi Rotterdam. In: Architectuur NL nr. 3, Doetinchem
	K. Theunissen: New Open Space in housing Ensembles. In: DASH. Rotterdam: NAi Publishers
	B. Leupen: Sequences between building and urban space. Le Medi Rotterdam. In: TBA-Time Based Architecture Volume 8. Gateshead UK: The Urban International Press
2010	J. Payne: James Payn profiles Holland's Geurst & Schulze. In : Brick Bulletin spring 2010. London: BDA- Brick Development Association
	B. Hulsman: De terugkeer van het Ornament. In: Kunst Schrift nr. 2, Amsterdam/Lochem
2011	Le Medi Rotterdam. In: Juryrapport Kleur Buiten Prijs 2010. Haarlem: Stichting Kleur Buiten
	I. Maglica: Scuola De Globetrotter a Rotterdam Olanda. In: Construire in Laterizio nr. 142- Edifici Scolastici. Milan Italy: Gruppo 24 Ore
	M. Hedman: The Need for Eco-humanism Dwelling. In: Ark 4/2011 Finnish Architectural Review, Helsinki.
2012	N. Yoshida: Architecture in the Netherlands. Le Medi – Geurst & Schulze architecten. In: A+U nr. 496. Tokyo: A+U Publishing
	B. Leupen/H. Mooij: Housing Design. A Manuel. Rotterdam: NAi Publishers
	P. Visser: Zorgvuldig ingepast met eigentijds karakter. In: Architectuur NL nr 02/2012. Doetinchem: Eisma Groep
	S. Meier: Multikultureller Wohnungsbau in den Niederlande. In: Bauwelt 12/12, Berlin.
	Yearbook 2012. Landscape architecture and Urban Design. Herinneringspark 2014-18, Wageningen: Blauwe Kamer/Blauwdruk

Diese Veröffentlichung ist mit finanzieller Unterstützung durch den Creative Industries Fund NL ermöglicht worden.

This publication was made possible through a grant from the Creative Industries Fund NL.

**creative industries
fund NL**

Quart Verlag Luzern/Quart Publishers Lucerne

De aedibus international
8 Dietrich | Untertrifaller (dt/e)
7 Geurst & Schulze Architecten (dt/e)
6 Wingender Hovenier Architecten (dt/e)
5 Tony Fretton Architects (dt/e)
4 Jonathan Woolf Architects (dt/e)
3 Hufnagel Pütz Rafaelian (dt/e)
2 Hild und K (dt/e)
1 Stanton Williams (dt/e)

Monografien / Monographs
Sergison Bates architects (dt und e)
Miroslav Šik. Architektur 1988–2012 (dt/e)
Valerio Olgiati (dt und e)
Burkard Meyer. Konkret/Concrete (dt/e)
Gion A. Caminada. Cul zuffel e l'aura dado (dt/e)

Quart Verlag GmbH, Heinz Wirz; Verlag für Architektur und Kunst
Denkmalstrasse 2, CH-6006 Luzern; books@quart.ch, www.quart.ch